OPPOSING
VIEWPOINTS®
SERIES

Tibet

Other Books of Related Interest:

Opposing Viewpoints Series
Culture Wars
Free Trade
Human Rights

At Issue Series
Does the World Hate the U.S.?
Should the U.S. Do Business With China?
U.S. Policy On Cuba

Current Controversies Series
Developing Nations
Illegal Immigration

"Congress shall make no law . . . abridging the freedom of speech, or of the press."

First Amendment to the U.S. Constitution

The basic foundation of our democracy is the First Amendment guarantee of freedom of expression. The Opposing Viewpoints Series is dedicated to the concept of this basic freedom and the idea that it is more important to practice it than to enshrine it.

OPPOSING VIEWPOINTS® SERIES

Tibet

Clare Hanrahan, Book Editor

GREENHAVEN PRESS
A part of Gale, Cengage Learning

GALE
CENGAGE Learning™

Detroit • New York • San Francisco • New Haven, Conn • Waterville, Maine • London

GALE
CENGAGE Learning

Christine Nasso, *Publisher*
Elizabeth Des Chenes, *Managing Editor*

© 2009 Greenhaven Press, a part of Gale, Cengage Learning.

Gale and Greenhaven Press are registered trademarks used herein under license.

For more information, contact:
Greenhaven Press
27500 Drake Rd.
Farmington Hills, MI 48331-3535
Or you can visit our Internet site at gale.cengage.com

LIBRARY OF CONGRESS CATALOGING-IN-PUBLICATION DATA

Tibet / Clare Hanrahan, book editor.
   p. cm. -- (Opposing viewpoints)
   Includes bibliographical references and index.
   ISBN-13: 978-0-7377-4240-4 (hardcover)
   ISBN-13: 978-0-7377-4241-1 (pbk.)
   1. Tibet (China)-- Politics and government--1951- 2. Self-determination, National-- China--Tibet. 3. Tibet (China)--Relations--China. 4. China--Relations--Tibet (China) 5. Ethnic groups--China--Tibet. I. Hanrahan, Clare.
   JQ1519.T553T53 2009
   951'.505--dc22

                                                                 2008036461

Printed in the United States of America
1 2 3 4 5 6 7 12 11 10 09 08

Contents

Chapter 3: Have the Tibetan People Benefited from Chinese Central Government?

Chapter 4: What Are The Major Threats to Survival of Tibet's Natural Environment?

Why Consider Opposing Viewpoints?

> *"The only way in which a human being can make some approach to knowing the whole of a subject is by hearing what can be said about it by persons of every variety of opinion and studying all modes in which it can be looked at by every character of mind. No wise man ever acquired his wisdom in any mode but this."*
>
> *John Stuart Mill*

In our media-intensive culture it is not difficult to find differing opinions. Thousands of newspapers and magazines and dozens of radio and television talk shows resound with differing points of view. The difficulty lies in deciding which opinion to agree with and which "experts" seem the most credible. The more inundated we become with differing opinions and claims, the more essential it is to hone critical reading and thinking skills to evaluate these ideas. Opposing Viewpoints books address this problem directly by presenting stimulating debates that can be used to enhance and teach these skills. The varied opinions contained in each book examine many different aspects of a single issue. While examining these conveniently edited opposing views, readers can develop critical thinking skills such as the ability to compare and contrast authors' credibility, facts, argumentation styles, use of persuasive techniques, and other stylistic tools. In short, the Opposing Viewpoints Series is an ideal way to attain the higher-level thinking and reading skills so essential in a culture of diverse and contradictory opinions.

In addition to providing a tool for critical thinking, Opposing Viewpoints books challenge readers to question their own strongly held opinions and assumptions. Most people form their opinions on the basis of upbringing, peer pressure, and personal, cultural, or professional bias. By reading carefully balanced opposing views, readers must directly confront new ideas as well as the opinions of those with whom they disagree. This is not to simplistically argue that everyone who reads opposing views will—or should—change his or her opinion. Instead, the series enhances readers' understanding of their own views by encouraging confrontation with opposing ideas. Careful examination of others' views can lead to the readers' understanding of the logical inconsistencies in their own opinions, perspective on why they hold an opinion, and the consideration of the possibility that their opinion requires further evaluation.

Evaluating Other Opinions

To ensure that this type of examination occurs, Opposing Viewpoints books present all types of opinions. Prominent spokespeople on different sides of each issue as well as well-known professionals from many disciplines challenge the reader. An additional goal of the series is to provide a forum for other, less known, or even unpopular viewpoints. The opinion of an ordinary person who has had to make the decision to cut off life support from a terminally ill relative, for example, may be just as valuable and provide just as much insight as a medical ethicist's professional opinion. The editors have two additional purposes in including these less known views. One, the editors encourage readers to respect others' opinions—even when not enhanced by professional credibility. It is only by reading or listening to and objectively evaluating others' ideas that one can determine whether they are worthy of consideration. Two, the inclusion of such viewpoints encourages the important critical thinking skill of objectively evaluating an author's credentials and bias. This evaluation will illuminate an author's reasons for taking a particular stance on an issue and will aid in readers' evaluation of the author's ideas.

It is our hope that these books will give readers a deeper understanding of the issues debated and an appreciation of the complexity of even seemingly simple issues when good and honest people disagree. This awareness is particularly important in a democratic society such as ours in which people enter into public debate to determine the common good. Those with whom one disagrees should not be regarded as enemies but rather as people whose views deserve careful examination and may shed light on one's own.

Thomas Jefferson once said that "difference of opinion leads to inquiry, and inquiry to truth." Jefferson, a broadly educated man, argued that "if a nation expects to be ignorant and free . . . it expects what never was and never will be." As individuals and as a nation, it is imperative that we consider the opinions of others and examine them with skill and discernment. The Opposing Viewpoints Series is intended to help readers achieve this goal.

David L. Bender and Bruno Leone,
Founders

Introduction

"Nowadays, Tibetan culture is being modernized and is open to the world. . . . It is embracing new momentum and demonstrating fresh and vigorous vitality. . . . A harmonious society and a harmonious world call for harmoniously coexisting cultures. The preservation and development of Tibetan culture is an important part of building an advanced socialist culture with Chinese characteristics and an unshirkable responsibility of the Chinese government."

—Liu Yandong,
vice chairwoman of the National
Committee of the Chinese People's
Political Consultative Conference

Tibet is a land with a culture and history imbued with myth, mystery, and strife. The country is strategically situated on a high plateau in central Asia. With elevations up to sixteen thousand feet, Tibet is known as the rooftop of the world. The Himalayas lie to the south, the Kunlun and Altun ranges to the north, the Karakoram to the west, and to the east are the high mountains of Szechwan. Deep lakes feed major rivers, including the Indus and the Ganges, that begin their flow high on the Tibetan plateau.

Traditional Tibet was a feudal theocracy under the spiritual leadership of the Dalai Lama. For centuries, Tibet remained a mostly hidden, secret place, geographically isolated from the rest of the world. Nomads herding livestock roamed the vast grasslands and serfs worked the land, supplying the needs of the large monasteries where powerful lamas, or Buddhist teachers, lived in relative luxury. Tibet remains an ethnically, culturally, religiously, and linguistically distinct region of the world, despite growing pressures of modernization and an influx of ethnic Chinese, known as Han, who emigrate to the Tibetan plateau where the wages they receive are higher and the air cleaner than in mainland China. China's push for modernization, which they have called "Opening and Development of the Western Regions," according to some critics, has led to exploitation of Tibet's considerable natural resources to supply China's industrial base.

To indigenous Tibetans, the land of Tibet is comprised of the three provinces of Amdo, Kham, and U-Tsang, which made up the territory of ancient Tibet prior to the Chinese takeover in 1959. To the ruling Chinese, Tibet is comprised only of the Tibet Autonomous Region (TAR), an area about the size of western Europe, designated by the Chinese government in 1965 and considered a part of the People's Republic of China. TAR is geographically less than half of the territory that comprised historical Tibet. It is recognized by the United States Department of State as a part of the People's Republic of China.

When the Dalai Lama fled his home in Lhasa, the capital of Tibet, in 1959 to escape the pursuing Chinese army, he sought political asylum in India. Tens of thousands of Tibetans left with him in an unprecedented exodus. These exiles formed the Tibetan Government in Exile, which operates from its headquarters in Dharamsala, India. Dharamsala established the first National Assembly in 1960, and in 2001, Professor Samdhong Rinpoche became the Tibetan Government in Exile's first elected Prime Minister. The exodus from the Tibetan plateau continues. In 2006, a reported 2,405 Tibetans arrived in Nepal at the Tibet Reception Center. Reports from fleeing Tibetans and human rights investigators tell of a brutal rule by the Chinese Communist Party (CCP) and of the use of imprisonment and torture to stifle dissent. Compounding the threat, some critics contend, is a looming environmental crisis.

"China is accustomed to reacting with brutality when its supremacy is threatened," writes Maura Moynihan, a former consultant with Refugees International. "Rapid growth has caused calamitous environmental damage that could lead to food shortages and unhygienic living and working conditions, which in turn could lead to epidemics and, eventually chaos."

The Tibet-China issue has been an ongoing and contentious one, particularly in recent years as growing numbers of Tibetans in exile clamor for independence, and many ethnic Tibetans who live under Chinese rule agitate for the return of the Dalai Lama and an end to what they experience as religious repression. Chinese officials distrust the Dalai Lama, ban display of his image, and insist that Chinese sovereignty is a matter of vital national interest. Safeguarding the unity of the motherland, they contend, is necessary for the harmonious society they seek.

Tibet's status as an independent nation is a matter of debate. The People's Republic of China claims Tibet as an "autonomous region" within the Chinese motherland. The long history of Tibet is recounted differently depending on the loyalties of the storyteller. China insists on its absolute claim to ownership of Tibet, while Tibet's growing movements for independence assert that Tibet was and remains a sovereign nation under occupation.

A 2008 editorial in *The Hindu*, an online edition of India's national newspaper, contends, "There is not a single government in the world that either disputes the status of Tibet; or does not recognize it as a part of the People's Republic of China; or is willing to accord any kind of legal recognition to the Dalai Lama's 'government-in-exile.'"

In *Opposing Viewpoints: Tibet*, many controversial aspects of the troubled relationship between Tibet and China are presented, as well as the ecological, demographic and economic stresses on the Tibetan plateau, and the modernization that could forever change the conditions of the indigenous inhabitants whose lives are so intimately bound with the land. The authors present differing viewpoints on the history of Tibet, the human rights and environmental protection afforded to its inhabitants, its governance, and its future within, or independent of, the People's Republic of China.

CHAPTER 1

Who Should Rule Tibet?

Chapter Preface

The cry "Free Tibet" garnered a good bit of press and airtime along the route of the 2008 official Beijing Olympic torch. China's troubled relationship with Tibet was headline news as Tibetan independence and human rights groups throughout the world took advantage of the prelude to China's Beijing Olympics to leverage publicity.

In 1950, the government of the People's Republic of China (PRC) engaged in either liberation or an armed invasion and occupation of Tibet, depending upon one's point of view. The Chinese military presence in Tibet is viewed by Beijing as democratic reform and by critics of the Chinese Communist Party's (CCP) top-down rule as repression and domination.

Among Tibetans, there are those who seek independence from China and those who seek genuine autonomy for Tibet within China. This rift has exposed a temperamental difference between the new generation of Tibetans, educated in exile and impatient with the status quo, and the Dalai Lama, Tibet's spiritual, and to some, temporal leader, who seeks what he calls the "Middle Way."

Tenzin Gyatso, the fourteenth Dalai Lama, fled Tibet in 1959 as the Chinese military advanced on his residence, the Potala Palace in Lhasa. Today, many thousands of Tibetans live in exile while others continue to flee the Tibetan plateau, despite dangerous restrictions on leaving. The Dalai Lama set up the Tibetan Government in Exile in Dharamsala, India, and on the Tibetan plateau, the Chinese Communist Party in 1965 established what is known as the Tibet Autonomous Region (TAR), representing only a fraction of the territory of ancient Tibet.

"On the future of Tibet, let me take this opportunity to restate categorically that I am not seeking independence. I am seeking a meaningful autonomy for the Tibetan people within the People's Republic of China," the Dalai Lama proclaimed in his acceptance speech in 2007 for the U.S. Congressional Gold Medal. "If the real concern of the Chinese leadership is the unity and stability of PRC, I have fully addressed their concerns. I have chosen to adopt this position because I believe, given the obvious benefits especially in economic development, this would be in the best interest of the Tibetan people. Furthermore, I have no intention of using any agreement on autonomy as a stepping stone for Tibet's independence."

Despite the Dalai Lama's insistence that a "Middle Way"—one that would assure genuine Tibetan autonomy within the People's Republic of China—is the most workable solution, the Chinese Central Government in Beijing remains both skeptical of the Dalai Lama and inclined toward harsh treatment of dissenters as the movements for Tibetan independence become more strident.

The Embassy of the People's Republic of China in the United States contends, "After the Dalai Lama went abroad, he was more closely surrounded and influenced by the former serf-owners and secessionists, and depended on others for subsistence. Since then, he has gone farther and farther on the path to betray his homeland and the people, becoming a tool of foreign anti-China forces and a chief representative of the 'Tibet independence' secessionist forces."

In a 2008 editorial calling on China to negotiate with the Dalai Lama, the *Dallas Morning News* wrote, "Neither Tibetan nationalists nor Chinese authorities can hope to win this fight with force. While there's still time, China should talk without guile to the Dalai Lama, a man of peace whose requests are reasonable."

In the following chapter, various authors present their views on the critical issue of who should rule Tibet. This issue is at the center of the debate on the fate of the unique and rapidly modernizing culture of the Tibetan Plateau. How Tibet is governed, and what Tibet's relationship with the People's

Republic of China will become, as well as the part the Dalai Lama and his Tibetan Government in Exile will play in negotiations, are questions of vital concern to the future of Tibet.

> "It is time for China to craft an approach that fully recognizes Tibet as a distinctive and valued national community within the PRC [People's Republic of China]."

China Should Acknowledge Tibetan Autonomy Within China

Michael C. Davis

Michael C. Davis is an author and professor of law at the Chinese University of Hong Kong where he is chair of the Human Rights Research Committee. His research topics include international law, the political economy of human rights, human rights and political culture, constitutionalism, and humanitarian intervention and the emerging global order. In the following viewpoint, Davis argues for a form of Tibetan autonomy within China that is appropriately grounded in China's Constitution and international human rights practice. He contends that this could "open the door to genuine and enduring solutions to this long-festering problem."

Michael C. Davis, "The Quest for Self-Rule in Tibet," *Journal of Democracy*, vol. 18, October, 2007, pp. 157–169. Copyright © 2007 The Johns Hopkins University Press. Reproduced by permission.

As you read, consider the following questions:

1. According to Davis, why would Article 31 of the 1982 Constitution of the People's Republic of China provide a workable alternative to the current national-minority policy?

2. What is the percentage of Han Chinese living in the People's Republic of China? What is the percentage of the other fifty-five national minorities, including Tibetans, who live in China?

3. According to Davis, which two circumstances "internationalize" Tibet's claim for internal autonomy? Does Davis consider these circumstances justified and legitimate?

The case of Tibet stands out as one of the most persistent and difficult human rights problems in the world today. Since the Dalai Lama fled Tibet in 1959, the Tibetan government-in-exile based in Dharamsala, India, and the government of the People's Republic of China (PRC) in Beijing have labored over this problem with no satisfactory result. Though the Chinese government has imposed its own version of "autonomy" under its national-minority policy, this version has achieved very little of what it promises. The Tibetan position has evolved from cries for independence in the early years of exile to calls for "genuine autonomy" today. The hope is that autonomy will promote the conditions necessary for participation in cultural, social, economic, and political life, promoting both democracy and human rights in Tibet.

China can best meet its acknowledged obligations to the Tibetan people by shifting away from its current application of the national-minority policy to a more flexible approach that opens the door to genuine negotiations. Practically, this move is already available under Article 31 of the PRC's 1982 Constitution, which is now being applied in Hong Kong. Article 31 says that "The state may establish special administrative regions when necessary. The systems to be instituted in special administrative regions shall be prescribed by law enacted by the National People's Congress [or NPC, China's legislature] in the light of the specific conditions."

Article 31's provision for the creation of "special administrative regions" allows a more tailored response to special cases than does the alternative national-minority approach now taken. . . .

A Cordial Dialogue

The Tibet problem has attracted renewed interest as Chinese officials and the Dalai Lama's representatives have engaged in six rounds of talks beginning in 2002. As a measure of their sincerity, exiled Tibetan leaders have urged their fellow exiles to show greater restraint in order to foster a "cordial atmosphere" for these discussions. Though both the Dalai Lama and Chinese officials report little progress, both sides appear to have appreciated the opportunity for dialogue. If nothing else, these talks have confirmed each side's bottom-line objective: For the Tibetans it is "genuine autonomy," while for China it is the PRC's "sovereignty" over Tibet. With political will, these objectives are ultimately reconcilable. The Tibetan leaders have advanced a "middle-way" approach that seeks genuine autonomy but abandons earlier calls for sovereign independence. The Chinese have responded with insistence on their existing national-minority policies, taking comfort in China's actual control of Tibet as a *fait accompli* [irreversible fact] as well as the international recognition that this state of affairs has achieved. These policies incorporate a form of top-down Chinese Communist Party (CCP) rule that makes genuine local autonomy difficult to achieve. For China, the assertion of its sovereignty over Tibet is a matter of vital national interest. Beijing shows little concern for the difficulties that the Tibetans face in negotiating with such a powerful adversary.

Important Components of the Middle-Way Approach

1. Without seeking independence for Tibet, the Central Tibetan Administration strives for the creation of a political entity comprising the three traditional provinces of Tibet;

2. Such an entity should enjoy a status of genuine national regional autonomy;

3. This autonomy should be governed by the popularly elected legislature and executive through a democratic process and should have an independent judicial system;

4. As soon as the above status is agreed upon by the Chinese government, Tibet would not seek separation from, and remain within, the People's Republic of China;

5. Until the time Tibet is transformed into a zone of peace and non-violence, the Chinese government can keep a limited number of armed forces in Tibet for its protection;

6. The Central Government of the People's Republic of China has the responsibility for the political aspects of Tibet's international relations and defense, whereas the Tibetan people should manage all other affairs pertain-ing to Tibet, such as religion and culture, education, economy, health, ecological and environmental protection;

7. The Chinese government should stop its policy of human rights violations in Tibet and the transfer of Chinese population into Tibetan areas;

8. To resolve the issue of Tibet, His Holiness the Dalai Lama shall take the main responsibility of sincerely pursuing negotiations and reconciliation with the Chinese government.

TibetNet, "The Middle-Way Approach: A Framework for Resolving the Issue of Tibet," March 17, 2008. www.Tibet.net.

A legacy of mistrust persists. Beginning in mid-2006 after the fifth meeting, Chinese officials put the discussions on hold for more than a year, offering increased criticism of the Dalai Lama. . . .

Chinese officials view Tibetans' loyalty to the Dalai Lama as a threat, but Beijing should also stop to ponder what this devotion suggests about the Dalai Lama's ability to marshal impressive popular support for an agreement. Speaking from India, Tibetan-exile activists such as Lobsang Yeshi, the vice-president of the pro-independence Tibetan Youth Congress, and Tenzin Tsundue, a prominent social activist, showed support for the Dalai Lama's efforts despite their own skepticism regarding the sincerity with which the PRC approaches autonomy discussions. Yeshi complains that Tibetans are allowed "talks about talks," but when they finally explain their position the PRC condemns them. As Karma Chophel, who chairs the legislative assembly of the Tibetan government-in-exile, has noted, skepticism about progress has grown within his own Assembly of Tibetan People's Deputies. Rato Ngawang, a former "Mustang" resistance fighter trained by the CIA and now a "middle-way" supporter, even wonders whether any agreement will have to wait until democracy replaces communism in China. The Dalai Lama may be the only person able to bridge these gaps and unite this weary community. At the same time, he offers the Chinese a rather agreeable negotiating partner. Many Chinese officials, nevertheless, appear to favor waiting until the 72-year-old Dalai Lama dies to "solve" the Tibet problem.

Vast Population Disparity

One cannot fully grasp the concerns of both sides without considering basic demographics. To begin with, there is the vast population disparity between the roughly 5.5 million Tibetans and the almost 1.2-billion-strong Han Chinese. (Tibetans who live in exile, mostly in India, number only about 130,000.) This problem is common to all 55 national minorities within the PRC, since together they make up just 8 percent of the overall population while the remaining 92 percent is Han. Taken together, the 13 geographical districts that the PRC has designated as Tibetan autonomous areas nearly approximate what Tibetans consider greater Tibet, and encompass about a quarter of the PRC's total land area. Demographic data regarding these Tibetan areas is disputed, as Tibetans in exile worry that China intends eventually to swamp the whole area with Han migrants. Official PRC census figures from 2000 (the most recent available) place the Han Chinese population in Tibetan areas at about 1.5 million. The Chinese figures for only the Tibet Autonomous Region (TAR)—the largest and western-most of all the designated Tibetan areas—claim approximately 2.5 million Tibetans and 160,000 Han Chinese. Scholars sometimes fault the Chinese census data for leaving out significant numbers of those residing temporarily in Tibet, including soldiers from the People's Liberation Army [PLA] and unregistered Han traders and workers. Chinese policies to encourage Han Chinese to "go west" to minority regions are seen as reflecting Beijing's desire to dominate the urban sector and assimilate Tibetans. Some conclude that the Chinese already form majorities in larger cities such as Lhasa and Xigaze.

China's existing policies, enacted under Article 4 of the PRC Constitution and the related national-minority laws, have failed to provide Tibetans with ultimate control over their own affairs, leaving the Tibetan community beleaguered and repressed. Since I take seriously both sides' expressed interest in internal autonomy rather than independence, I will leave the issue of independence aside. The historic Chinese rejection of the more flexible approach to autonomy available under Article 31 is unjustified and fails to appreciate both the history of China's centuries-long relationship with Tibet and the gravity of the PRC's international obligations. The choice of this alternative could open the door to genuine and enduring solutions to this long-festering problem. . . .

China's minority policy in Tibet further rests on fictions such as the notion that the PRC's 1950 armed invasion and subsequent occupation of the region were acts of "liberation" that brought about "democratic reform" in the shape of CCP rule. According to Beijing's Marxist logic, colonialism can only be a product of capitalism and hence could not have been committed by the PRC. Under this theory, the exploited classes of Tibet would be joined with other Chinese in a common program of local autonomous rule. This "common program" saw the autonomy arrangement as merely a step on the way to the assimilation of minorities into the dominant Han Chinese state. For instance, although the seventeen-point agreement which China largely forced upon the Tibetan government after the PLA invasion promised that Beijing "would not alter the existing political system in Tibet," China clearly envisioned that—and behaved as if—the liberated Tibetans would soon favor "reform," meaning the CCP's vision of minority autonomy. . . .

China's Policies Have Failed

The current approach is a failure that serves neither China's interests nor the Tibetan people's needs. China's policies toward Tibet have failed to match its traditional obligations, reflected in centuries of distinctive Sino-Tibetan relations, and have likewise failed to meet its minimum international responsibilities to an autonomous national community. It is time for China to craft an approach that fully recognizes Tibet as a distinctive and valued national community within the PRC. . . .

Beijing sees continued control over Tibet as a matter of vital national interest. Under such circumstances, *fait accompli* has combined with *realpolitik* [advancement of the national interest] to deny Tibetans any hope of independence. Given all this, is there any international legal security for the internal autonomy that the Tibetans now seek?

While guarantees of autonomy have generally not been well secured by international law, it may be argued that under at least two circumstances autonomy in effect becomes internationalized: 1) when it is the consequence of treaty arrangements transferring or surrendering sovereignty, or 2) when it arises out of the denial of rights of self-determination. The Tibet case may implicate both possibilities. There has been steady foreign pressure on Beijing since the 1950s to live up to the commitments that it has made to Tibetan autonomy. Given the historical circumstances, such solicitude appears justified and legitimate. . . .

Current expressions of recognition of China's claims to Tibet are generally thought to depend on the sheer weight that China can throw around in world affairs. An autonomy arrangement with a level of democracy and human rights acceptable to the Dalai Lama and the government-in-exile may encourage more genuine local and international satisfaction with Chinese sovereignty in Tibet.

"The so-called 'enlarged Tibet autonomous region' runs counter to the law that governs the development of various ethnic groups in China. If all of the 55 ethnic minorities founded their own unified autonomous areas, there would [be] conflicts between various ethnic groups and social disorder in China."

China Should Not Acknowledge Tibetan Autonomy Within China

Yedor

Yedor is a writer for the Web site of the Beijing-based China Tibet Information Center, an extensive multilanguage Web site publishing news and information about Tibet from the point of view of the Chinese Central Government. In the following viewpoint, Yedor contends that an "enlarged Tibet autonomous region" would conflict with China's Constitution that prohibits any sabotage of national unity. Such Tibetan autonomy, in Yedor's view, would also violate China's Law on National Regional Autonomy, which asserts that all ethnic groups should enjoy equal rights.

Yedor, "On the 'Middle Way' of the Dalai Lama," *China Tibet Information Center*, July 18, 2006. Reproduced by permission.

As you read, consider the following questions:

1. Yedor contends that the Dalai Lama has an "ulterior motive" for seeking autonomy within China. In Yedor's view, what is the Dalai Lama up to?

2. When were the Dalai Lama's five- and seven-point principles first proposed? In Yedor's opinion, who influenced the Dalai Lama regarding the five points?

3. According to Yedor, what did the Dalai Lama tell a French reporter that the young people would do if he failed in negotiations with the Chinese government?

Following the founding of the PRC [People's Republic of China] in 1949, eight Tibetan autonomous prefectures, one Tibetan-Qiang autonomous prefecture, one Mongolian-Tibetan autonomous prefecture, and two Tibetan autonomous counties were established. Such administrative division is made in accordance with the features of various ethnic groups and with the aim of seeking future development; it embodies factors related to ethnic groups and regions as well, the integration of political and economic factors; hence, it is good for the ethnic groups concerned to seek common development within the big Chinese family.

From this we see the so-called "enlarged Tibet autonomous region" runs counter to the law that governs the development of various ethnic groups in China. If all of the 55 ethnic minorities founded their own unified autonomous areas, there would [be] conflicts between various ethnic groups and social disorder in China, all these would be a bane for the economic and cultural development of these ethnic groups. One can not see much relations between the "enlarged Tibet autonomous region" and efforts to protect the Tibetan features. However, it is easy for one to see the Dalai Lama's ulterior motive: eventually seeking Tibetan independence.

At the end of [2005], when the Dalai Lama was interviewed by reporters, he said: "Tibet enjoys the right to special treatment in accordance with the Law on National Regional Autonomy", but "this right has not been really enjoyed". Sangdong, the chief Galoon ["Premier"] of the Tibetan government-in-exile recently said that "the policy of the national regional autonomy is very important, but the Chinese government lacks fairness in following the policy, which does not conform to the Law on National Regional Autonomy". They impress people that the Dalai Lama favors the national regional autonomy but wishes to see the fulfillment of various rights specified in the law.

A Tibetan "Peace Zone?"

What is the Dalai Lama up to? Here are two examples: In the "five points", he said: "The course of real peace can only begin when the Communist troops have all pulled out". In his "seven points," he said: "A regional peace conference should be convened to guarantee demilitarization in Tibet". Recently, the Dalai Lama entrusted a professor in Hong Kong to draft a document called "limitations and possibilities of achieving 'high-level autonomy' within the framework of the Chinese Constitution and the Law on National Regional Autonomy", which outlines a Tibetan "peace zone" where "no troops should be deployed". But it is well known in the world that deploying troops in its own territories is a requirement of national defense and also a symbol of sovereignty. Withdrawing its troops from its own territory so as to turn that part of its territory into a "peace zone" will not be approved by any country upholding its sovereignty and dignity in the world. Neither will China. From this, we see the "high-level autonomy" the Dalai Lama pursues is empty-worded.

Equal Rights for All Ethnic Groups

The other example is one related to the relations between various ethnic groups in areas following the national regional autonomy system. Article 4 of the PRC Constitution says all

The Case Against Autonomy for Tibet

Why does the Tibetan Government-In-Exile (TGIE) ask for autonomy for Tibet from Communist China that would give Tibetans considerably less freedom than those of us in exile currently enjoy? Presently, we are free to worship, voice our opinion on political and national issues, travel, practice and promote our religion, culture and traditions, and free to even vote for our Parliament-in-Exile. Why would the TGIE seek an agreement that denies such rights to us?

As for those living in Tibet, as the Dalai Lama himself has said, they may be somewhat enjoying the benefits of Communist China's economic progress, except that they cannot practice their own culture, seek independence or engage in any activity against the Communist Chinese regime. But what use is "autonomy" if it means restricting our unique cultural, religious and peaceful political activities?. . .

By asking the Communist Chinese for an official agreement to have autonomous status for Tibet, we will be surrendering many of the rights we are now entitled to and locking ourselves into a constricted and precarious situation forever from which we cannot withdraw.

Tsoltim N. Shakabba,
"The Case Against Autonomy for Tibet,"
January 14, 2008. www.tibetanavenue.com.

ethnic groups in the PRC are equal, and no one is allowed to discriminate against and suppress any ethnic group, sabotage national unity, and engage in national separation. Article 48 of the Law on National Regional Autonomy also stipulates that the organ responsible for autonomy in areas exercising national regional autonomy shall work to guarantee all local ethnic groups enjoy equal rights. However, the Dalai Lama said in his "five points" that the Central Government "must stop moving people into Tibet and Han people already in Tibet must return to China." Sangdong also said last year [2005] that "the areas where the Tibetans reside should have Tibetans exercising regional national autonomy, and the Han and other ethnic groups should act like guests and Tibetans' rights should not be restricted in any form." All people with knowledge of Chinese history know the areas at the rim of the so-called "enlarged Tibetan area", especially the rim of the Qinghai-Tibet Plateau, formed a region witnessing considerable movement of peoples and where Tibetans, Han, Hui, and Mongolians eventually came to live together and rely on each other. They are all masters of the areas where they live. Making non-Tibetans move away from where they have lived for many centuries, so as to satisfy the Dalai Lama, goes against the PRC Constitution and the Law on National Regional Autonomy, and shows that, once the Dalai Lama becomes leader of Tibet again, he will follow policies featuring national discrimination and national purge. Such a policy caused heavy deaths in the mid-20th century in some countries and the Dalai Lama should know this.

From the above analysis, we see the Dalai Lama is talking about seeking a way out "within the framework of the Chinese Constitution" but, at the same time, he sticks to his principles that run counter to the PRC Constitution. This shows that what he pursues is a swindle and nothing stands between his "high-level autonomy" and "Tibetan independence". When the Dalai Lama made public his "five points" and "seven points", the Central Government immediately made it clear that this showed he had not given up his stand for "independence of Tibet". Any form of "independence of Tibet" won't do. In 1987, a US congressional source declared: "The United States has not shown any support for the Dalai's five points geared to turn Tibet into a peace zone, as behind them is the obvious intention to promote Tibetan independence". The Tibetan Bulletin operated by the Dalai clique carried a signed story in 2004 saying: 'Elements who stand for independence think the five-point peace proposal and the Strasbourg proposal are a kind of betrayal, because they have failed to read between lines. So long as conditions are ripe, they will play a role geared to gaining real independence.'

The five and seven points are what the Dalai Lama first proposed some 20 years ago. Some may say he did so at that time because he was under the strong influence of foreign anti-China forces; but what he proposes as the "middle way" is something different. This writer has been examining a "publicity pamphlet" on the middle way issued in June 2005 by the "foreign affairs and news relations department of the Tibet government-in-exile". Highlights of the "manual on the middle way" show it to be closely related to the five and seven points. The manual says the Strasbourg proposal was put forward by the Dalai Lama and determined in a democratic way and hence should not be altered. Sangdong told Tibetans who went to India from China for Buddhist rituals in 2005 that "all the work should be done on the basis of the 1987 five points and 1988 Strasbourg proposal of the Dalai Lama. They are our political program".

It is true that when the Dalai dished out his five and seven points, he was under foreign influence. In June 1987, US House of Representatives proposed a revision regarding human rights in Tibet, which was the first Western resolution against China related to Tibet in the 1980s. In September the same year, the Dalai Lama visited the United States ostensibly as a religious leader. He dished out his "five points" at a US human rights group meeting on September 21. Some reported that the "five-point" speech was drafted by people within the US group according to the US document entitled "Revised Scheme on Human Rights in Tibet". The American scholar [Melvyn C.] Goldstein pointed out in his work *Dragon and the Snow Lion* that the new offensive launched by the Dalai government-in-exile and its friends in London, New York and Washington, D.C., was meant for Western audiences, instead of the Chinese. . . .

A Blind Alley

In 2003, [the Dalai Lama] told a French reporter: "If no results can be achieved in two or three years of negotiations, I would find it hard to explain to the young that the 'middle way' is more effective than seeking independence"; "if I fail, these young people would raise torches and cry for independence". Given the fact that the Dalai Lama gives out different signals at different times and even at the same time, one can hardly agree his "middle way" is different from "Tibetan independence".

As a matter of fact, the "middle way" is a philosophy, according to which one should not take extreme actions. But the Dalai's "middle way" has nothing to do with the "middle way" philosophy. The Central Government has made public its views on the Dalai's "middle way" over the past 20 years, but the Dalai Lama still hates to say bye to his proposals which are "independence of Tibet" in nature. It left no stone unturned to bargain with the Central Government by changing words. This writer holds that the Dalai Lama is in a blind alley. We Tibetans value highly the Sagya Sayings, which says: "One should refrain from thinking to do things one could not do; and eat food which can hardly be digested;" "a fool takes a wrong way, simply because he is a fool; when a wiseman takes a wrong way, he must find out the why." If the Dalai Lama is sincere in improving ties with the Central Government, he needs, first and foremost, to have an objective understanding of the political reality in Tibet and, on this basis, re-think his political propositions. Only by truly giving up his "Tibetan independence" policy, can the Dalai Lama win the confidence of others and create conditions for him to do something in the interest of Tibet.

> *"The battle for Tibetan independence was lost 49 years ago when the Dalai Lama escaped into exile. His goal, and that of those who want to help the Tibetan people, should be to negotiate realistically with the Chinese state. The present protests, supported from overseas, will bring only more suffering."*

The Exiled Government of the Dalai Lama Should Try to Negotiate with China

Patrick French

Patrick French is the author of the book Tibet, Tibet: A Personal History of a Lost Land. *French first met the Dalai Lama when the Tibetan leader visited his school in northern England. This led to French's lifelong study of Tibet and its people. French is a former director of the Free Tibet movement, and also edited the bulletin* Tibet News. *In the following viewpoint, French contends that popular internationalization of the Tibet issue is not helping the Tibetan people. He argues that the Dalai Lama should have publicly renounced the claim to a so-called Greater Tibet as a move toward realistic negotiation with China.*

Patrick French, "He May Be a God, But He's No Politician," *The New York Times*, March 22, 2008. Copyright © 2008 by Patrick French, reprinted with permission of The Wylie Agency, Inc.

As you read, consider the following questions:

1. What was the response of Tibetan monks to the Dalai Lama's award of the Congressional Gold Medal?

2. In French's view, how does the Dalai Lama's political philosophy of a "middle way" compare with Mahatma Gandhi's philosophy of nonviolent resistance?

3. Why is the popular internationalization of Tibet not having a positive effect on the Beijing government, according to French?

Nearly a decade ago, while staying with a nomad family in the remote grasslands of northeastern Tibet, I asked Namdrub, a man who fought in the anti-Communist resistance in the 1950s, what he thought about the exiled Tibetans who campaigned for his freedom. "It may make them feel good, but for us, it makes life worse," he replied. "It makes the Chinese create more controls over us. Tibet is too important to the Communists for them even to discuss independence."

Protests have spread across the Tibetan plateau over the last two weeks [March 2008], and at least 100 people have died. Anyone who finds it odd that [U.S. House] Speaker Nancy Pelosi has rushed to Dharamsala, India, to stand by the Dalai Lama's side fails to realize that American politics provided an important spark for the demonstrations. Last October [2007], when the Congressional Gold Medal was awarded to the Dalai Lama, monks in Tibet watched over the Internet and celebrated by setting off fireworks and throwing barley flour. They were quickly arrested.

It was for the release of these monks that demonstrators initially turned out this month. Their brave stand quickly metamorphosed into a protest by Lhasa residents who were angry that many economic advantages of the last 10 or 15 years had gone to Han Chinese and Hui Muslims. A young refugee whose family is still in Tibet told me this week of the medal, "People believed that the American government was

Dialogue: The Only Means of Resolution

The Chinese authorities criticize us for internationalizing the Tibet issue. But the fact of the matter is that Tibet became an international issue from the beginning precisely because of Chinese actions. The only remedy in front of us is to resolve the issue through dialogue. . . .

Now is the time for a resolution to this issue. I hope the Chinese leadership seizes this opportunity. His Holiness is widely recognized and admired for his honesty and integrity. He has been pragmatic and flexible in wanting to negotiate with the leadership in Beijing on the kind of status Tibet should enjoy in the future, and has held steadfast to his commitment to non-violence and dialogue as the only means of resolving the issue of Tibet. . . .

His Holiness's world view, his special bond with the Tibetan people, and the respect he enjoys in the international community all make the person of His Holiness key both to achieving a negotiated solution to the Tibetan issue and to peacefully implementing any agreement that is reached. This is why I have consistently conveyed to my Chinese counterparts that far from being the problem, His Holiness is the solution.

Lodi G. Gyari, "Testimony of Lodi G. Gyari, Special Envoy of H.H. the Dalai Lama at House Foreign Affairs Committee Hearing on Status of Tibet Negotiations," March 13, 2007.

genuinely considering the Tibet issue as a priority." In fact, the award was a symbolic gesture, arranged mostly to make American lawmakers feel good.

A similar misunderstanding occurred in 1987 when the Dalai Lama was denounced by the Chinese state media for putting forward a peace proposal on Capitol Hill. To Tibetans brought up in the Communist system—where a politician's physical proximity to the leadership on the evening news indicates to the public that he is in favor—it appeared that the world's most powerful government was offering substantive political backing to the Dalai Lama. Protests began in Lhasa, and martial law was declared. The brutal suppression that followed was orchestrated by the party secretary in Tibet, Hu Jintao, who is now the Chinese president. His response to the current unrest is likely to be equally uncompromising.

A Poorly Advised Political Strategist

The Dalai Lama is a great and charismatic spiritual figure, but a poor and poorly advised political strategist. When he escaped into exile in India in 1959, he declared himself an admirer of Mahatma Gandhi's nonviolent resistance. But Gandhi took huge gambles, starting the Salt March and starving himself nearly to death—a very different approach from the Dalai Lama's "middle way," which concentrates on nonviolence rather than resistance. The Dalai Lama has never really tried to use direct action to leverage his authority.

At the end of the 1980s, he joined forces with Hollywood and generated huge popular support for the Tibetan cause in America and Western Europe. This approach made some sense at the time. The Soviet Union was falling apart, and many people thought China might do the same. In practice, however, the campaign outraged the nationalist and xenophobic Chinese leadership.

It has been clear since the mid-1990s that the popular internationalization of the Tibet issue has had no positive effect on the Beijing government. The leadership is not amenable to "moral pressure," over the Olympics or anything else, particularly by the nations that invaded Iraq.

Close Down the Hollywood Strategy

The Dalai Lama should have closed down the Hollywood strategy a decade ago and focused on back-channel diplomacy with Beijing. He should have publicly renounced the claim to a so-called Greater Tibet, which demands territory that was never under the control of the Lhasa government. Sending his envoys to talk about talks with the Chinese while simultaneously encouraging the global pro-Tibet lobby has achieved nothing.

When Beijing attacks the "Dalai clique," it is referring to the various groups that make Chinese leaders lose face each time they visit a Western country. The International Campaign for Tibet, based in Washington, is now a more powerful and effective force on global opinion than the Dalai Lama's outfit in northern India. The European and American pro-Tibet organizations are the tail that wags the dog of the Tibetan government-in-exile.

These groups hate criticism almost as much as the Chinese government does. Some use questionable information. For example, the Free Tibet Campaign in London (of which I am a former director) and other groups have long claimed that 1.2 million Tibetans have been killed by the Chinese since they invaded in 1950. However, after scouring the archives in Dharamsala while researching my book on Tibet, I found that there was no evidence to support that figure. The question that Nancy Pelosi and celebrity advocates like Richard Gere ought to answer is this: Have the actions of the Western pro-Tibet lobby over the last 20 years brought a single benefit to the Tibetans who live inside Tibet, and if not, why continue with a failed strategy?

I first visited Tibet in 1986. The economic plight of ordinary people is slightly better now, but they have as little political freedom as they did two decades ago. Tibet lacks genuine autonomy, and ethnic Tibetans are excluded from positions of real power within the bureaucracy or the army. Tibet was effectively a sovereign nation at the time of the Communist invasion and was in full control of its own affairs. But the battle for Tibetan independence was lost 49 years ago when the Dalai Lama escaped into exile. His goal, and that of those who want to help the Tibetan people, should be to negotiate realistically with the Chinese state. The present protests, supported from overseas, will bring only more suffering. China is not a democracy, and it will not budge.

"*[The Dalai Lama's] government-in-exile is illegal. . . . There are no talks between the Chinese and his so-called government-in-exile.*"

China Should Not Negotiate with the Exiled Government of the Dalai Lama

Der Spiegel

Der Spiegel, Germany's national news magazine, has been published weekly in Hamburg, Germany for more than fifty years. It provides news, analysis, and opinion on international topics. In this interview with Zhang Qingli, head of the Communist Party in Tibet, Zhang contends that the Dalai Lama has destabilized Tibet and seeks a return to an earlier, theocratic feudal realm. Negotiations will be open, Zhang contends, only when the Dalai Lama abandons claims to independence that would divide the motherland.

As you read, consider the following questions:

1. According to Zhang, what steps did the Chinese government take to guarantee religious freedom in Tibet?

"Dalai Lama Deceived His Motherland," *Der Spiegel,* August 16, 2006. www.spiegel.de. Reproduced by permission.

2. In Zhang's opinion, what does the Dalai Lama's "middle path" mean? What term does Zhang use to describe this position?

3. In Zhang's view, do many people really know the true Dalai Lama? Who are some of his supporters, according to Zhang?

SPIEGEL [national news magazine in Germany]: The Dalai Lama is one of the world's most popular religious leaders, and he is deeply revered by the people of Tibet. But the government in Beijing sees him as a despicable separatist. Why?

Zhang [Qingli, head of the Communist Party in Tibet]: Our policy toward the Dalai Lama is clear and consistent. After the founding of the People's Republic and the peaceful liberation of Tibet, he was elected to a leadership position in the National People's Congress in 1954. He remained a member of that body until 1964. In 1956, he was named director of the preparation committee for the Tibet Autonomous Region. All of this was done so that religious freedom could be guaranteed, and so that Tibet could be integrated into the great family of socialist nations. He fled the country in 1959. There is no doubt that at that time he was a widely respected religious leader.

SPIEGEL: And is he no longer that today?

Zhang: He did many bad things later on that contradict the role of a religious leader. The core issue is this: Everyone must love his motherland. How can it be that he doesn't even love his motherland? We have a saying: "No dog sees the filth in his own hut, and a son would never describe his mother as ugly."

SPIEGEL: The Dalai Lama doesn't love Tibet?

Zhang: Tibet is the home of the 14th Dalai Lama, but China is his motherland. He deceived his motherland. He rebelled in the 1950s and in the late 1980s he incited unrest in

Dalai Lama Has Betrayed His Motherland

For decades, the Dalai Lama has betrayed his motherland, engaged in separatist activities overseas and never given up his separatist political position. While continuing to engage in separatist activities and undermine China's relations with certain countries, he has been attempting to create a disguise for himself by talking about giving up "Tibet independence," and seeking only "high degree of autonomy" in recent years in order to win over international sympathy and support. The sabotaging activities that took place in Lhasa and other places recently were another direct exposure of the separatist position of the Dalai clique. We hope that the international community will come to a correct judgment and conclusion.

Embassy of the People's Republic of China
in the United States of America, "Press Release:
Facts About the Violent Sabotage in Lhasa of Tibet
and Other Places by 'Tibet Independence' Elements,"
March 18, 2008. www.china-embassy.org.

Lhasa that was directed against the people, the government and society. He destabilized Tibet.

SPIEGEL: The Dalai Lama is widely respected worldwide.

Zhang: If I remember correctly, from 1959 to the middle of this year [2006] he has made 312 visits to places all over the world, which comes to an average of six countries a year. It was even 12 in 2005. And what did he do during these visits? The goal of these so-called official visits was to form alliances with anti-Chinese forces and to engage in propaganda for his separatist views, which conflict with religion.

SPIEGEL: But much has changed in the world in the last 20 years. China has opened up and trade has become globalized. The question of power on the roof of the world has been resolved. The Dalai Lama has abandoned his claims to independence and agrees to a far-reaching autonomy for Tibet. Why isn't China generous and self-confident enough to allow the Dalai Lama back into the country, as he would like? Does he still pose a threat to you?

Zhang: We have a clear policy. The door to negotiations will always be open to him, but only when he truly and comprehensively abandons his intentions to divide the motherland, intentions that are directed against society and the people, only when he gives up his splittist activities and only when he openly declares to the world that he has given up claims to independence for Tibet.

SPIEGEL: Didn't he do this long ago?

Zhang: The problem is that his behavior and his statements contradict one another. He says: "I want to take a middle path and I accept that there is only one China." But in reality he has not spent a single day not trying to split the motherland.

SPIEGEL: What do you mean by that?

Zhang: What his so-called middle path means is this: He wants to integrate Tibetan settlement areas in the provinces of Sichuan, Yunnan, Qinghai and Gansu into Tibet. He wants to be in charge of this "Greater Tibet" and he demands that the People's Liberation Army be withdrawn from the region. Besides, he wants to see a return to an earlier, theocratic feudal realm, as dark and gruesome as it was. In those days, government officials, noblemen, and monks ruled 95 percent of the population. And he wants even more autonomy for Tibet than has been given to Hong Kong and Macau. That is splittism.

SPIEGEL: But haven't there already been talks between representatives of the Dalai Lama and Beijing?

Zhang: His government-in-exile is illegal. Our central government has never recognized it. No country in the world, including Germany, recognizes it diplomatically. There are no

talks between the Chinese and his so-called government-in-exile. The current contacts merely involve a few individuals from his immediate surroundings. The talks revolve around his personal future.

SPIEGEL: The Dalai Lama enjoys a great deal of sympathy in America, Europe and in Asia, also because the Chinese Communist Party is not particularly democratic.

Zhang: Frankly, the number of people who know the true Dalai Lama is very small. His supporters include enemies of China, but also the true faithful, who are being led astray by this false religious leader. And, finally, there are those who do not understand the real situation.

SPIEGEL: Nevertheless, the Dalai Lama is a winner of the Nobel Peace Prize.

Zhang: [I have not] understood why a person like the Dalai Lama was honored with this prize. What has he done for peace? How much guilt does he bear toward the Tibetan people! How damaging is he for Tibet and China! I cannot understand why so many countries are interested in him.

> "At the time when Chinese troops invaded Tibet in 1949, Tibet was an independent nation. Tibet had its own government, its own language, its own currency, its own postal system and its own legal system."

Tibet Is a Sovereign Nation Entitled to Self-Determination

Students for a Free Tibet

Students for a Free Tibet (SFT) is a nonprofit, student-led organization formed in 1994 to educate, advocate, and act to advance the cause of the Tibetan people and empower and train youth leaders. The international headquarters is in New York. Through a chapter-based worldwide network, students participate in campaigns for a free and independent Tibet. In the following viewpoint, SFT argues that the exiled Dalai Lama is the rightful leader of Tibet, and that the Tibetan people have maintained a spirit of resistance since the Chinese occupation—an occupation they contend is both illegal and brutal.

As you read, consider the following questions:

1. According to the Students for a Free Tibet, what term do the Chinese officials use to designate the region they call Tibet? When was this region created, and why?

2. In the authors' view, what circumstances compelled the Tibetan government to sign the 17-Point Agreement? When was this document signed?

3. How many Tibetans have lost their lives, according to the authors, as a result of the Chinese occupation?

Tibet lies at the center of Asia, with an area of 2.5 million square kilometers. The earth's highest mountains, a vast arid plateau and great river valleys make up the physical homeland of 6 million Tibetans. It has an average altitude of 14,000 feet above sea level.

Tibet is comprised of the three provinces of Amdo (now split by China into the provinces of Qinghai and part of Gansu), Kham (largely incorporated into the Chinese provinces of Sichuan, Gansu and Yunnan), and U-Tsang (which, together with western Kham, is today referred to by China as the Tibet Autonomous Region).

The Tibet Autonomous Region (TAR) comprises less than half of historic Tibet and was created by China in 1965 for administrative reasons. It is important to note that when Chinese officials and publications use the term "Tibet" they mean only the TAR.

Tibetans use the term Tibet to mean the three provinces described above, i.e., the area traditionally known as Tibet before the 1949–50 invasion.

Despite over 40 years of Chinese occupation of Tibet, the Tibetan people refuse to be conquered and subjugated by China. The present Chinese policy, a combination of demographic and economic manipulation, and discrimination, aims to suppress the Tibetan issue by changing the very character and the identity of Tibet and its people.

Today Tibetans are outnumbered by Han Chinese population in their own homeland. . . .

The Invasion of Tibet

The turning point in Tibet's history came in 1949, when the People's Liberation Army of the PRC [People's Republic of China] first crossed into Tibet. After defeating the small Tibetan army and occupying half the country, the Chinese government, in May 1951, imposed the so-called "17-Point Agreement for the Peaceful Liberation of Tibet" on the Tibetan government. Because it was signed under duress, the agreement lacked validity under international law. The presence of 40,000 troops in Tibet, the threat of the immediate occupation of Lhasa, and the prospect of the total obliteration of the Tibetan state, left Tibetans little choice.

As open resistance to the Chinese occupation escalated, particularly in eastern Tibet, the Chinese repression, which included the destruction of religious buildings and the imprisonment of monks and other community leaders, increased dramatically. By 1959, popular uprisings culminated in massive demonstrations in Lhasa. By the time China crushed the uprising, 87,000 Tibetans were dead in the Lhasa region alone, and the Dalai Lama had fled to India, where he now resides with the Tibetan Government in Exile. In 1963, the Dalai Lama promulgated a constitution for a democratic Tibet. It has been successfully implemented, to the extent possible, by the government in exile.

The Spirit to Resist

Meanwhile, in Tibet, religious persecution, consistent violations of human rights, and the wholesale destruction of religious and historic buildings by the occupying authorities have not succeeded in destroying the spirit of the Tibetan people to resist the destruction of their national identity. 1.2 million Tibetans have lost their lives (more than one sixth of the

Self-Determination Is the Right of Tibetan People

Self-determination has preeminent status in human rights law: it has been treated as the most basic of rights. The United Nations [UN] Charter, which China ratified, provides in Article 1 that the purpose of the UN is to "develop friendly relations among nations based on respect for the principles of equal rights and self-determination of peoples."

Furthermore, when the UN General Assembly produced the Declaration on Principles of International Law, listing the seven principles it considered most basic to relationships between nations, the list included "the principle of equal rights and self-determination of peoples."

Are the Tibetans a people, such that they would have a right of self-determination separate from the right of the other citizens of China? This is not a trivial question because there is no generally accepted legal definition of a people. However, the UN's primary experts on the subject are arguably the members of the Sub-Commission on Prevention of Discrimination and Protection of Minorities of the Commission on Human Rights. The Sub-Commission has acknowledged the Tibetans as a distinct people. Its resolution 1991/10, titled "Situation in Tibet," referred to the "distinct cultural, religious and national identity of the Tibetan people," in connection with calling upon the Chinese government to respect fully the Tibetans' fundamental rights.

Margit Roos-Collins, "The Legal Status of Tibet and China's International Responsibilities in Managing Tibet's Environment: Using Law and Politics to Protect Tibet's Environment," Tibet Justice Center, April 3, 2008. www.tibetjustice.org.

population) as a result of the Chinese occupation. But the new generation of Tibetans are just as determined to regain the country's independence as the older generation was. . . .

Tibet is an occupied country. This is the most important fact to remember when working for Tibetan freedom. We are not simply working for human rights or religious freedom in Tibet, we are working to free a nation from an illegal and brutal foreign occupation. At the time when Chinese troops invaded Tibet in 1949, Tibet was an independent nation. Tibet had its own government, its own language, its own currency, its own postal system and its own legal system. When we say "Free Tibet," we don't just mean, "Make things better in Tibet." We mean, "Free the nation of Tibet from Chinese occupation."

China's People's Liberation Army took Tibet by force. When Chairman Mao came to power in 1949, one of the first things he did was send his troops to annex Tibet. Tibet did not have a large or well-equipped army. While there was a determined armed resistance to the Chinese invasion, the relatively small Tibetan army was eventually crushed by the Chinese army. An agreement was imposed on the Tibetan government in May of 1951, acknowledging sovereignty over Tibet, but recognizing the Tibetan government's autonomy with respect to Tibet's internal affairs. As the Chinese consolidated their control, they repeatedly violated the treaty and open resistance to their rule grew.

Dalai Lama Is the Rightful Leader

By 1959, the situation had become dire in Tibet. Thousands of Tibetan refugees poured into western Tibet from the east, where Tibetan resistance fighters were engaged in open battle with the Chinese army. Massive demonstrations broke out in Lhasa, Tibet's capital, when rumors that the Dalai Lama's life was in danger began to circulate. Tenzin Gyatso, Tibet's 14th Dalai Lama, is the spiritual and political leader of Tibet. In

1959, he was only 24 years old. On March 10th 1959, hundreds of thousands of Tibetans massed around the Norbulingka Palace, the Dalai Lama's summer residence, to prevent him from attending an event to which the Chinese authorities had invited him. They feared he might be killed secretively. The demonstrators called for Tibetan independence and for Chinese forces to leave Tibet. When the situation became tense, the Dalai Lama fled under cover of darkness on March 17, 1959 to India, where he has lived since. Tens of thousands of Tibetans were killed by Chinese forces who broke up the mass protests.

Since 1959, Tibet has been solely under Chinese rule. The Tibetan people, both inside Tibet and in exile, long for the Dalai Lama to return to Tibet to resume his rightful place as Tibet's leader.

While the ultimate goal of Students for a Free Tibet is to help Tibetans regain their independent nation, we also work hard to end the atrocious violations of the Tibetan people's political, religious, cultural, social and economic rights by the Chinese government. However, it is important to bear in mind that we work in solidarity with the Tibetan people, who continue to struggle for the restoration of their country Tibet.

> "If western states, and the citizens of those states, wish to condemn China's sovereignty over Tibet, then for such criticism to be valid, it must be applied in equal measure to the sovereignty of the US, Canada, Mexico, and to the other countries on down to Tierra del Fuego."

Tibet Is Not Sovereign and Does Not Have an Absolute Right to Self-Determination

Kim Petersen

Kim Petersen is coeditor and contributing writer to the internet newsletter Dissident Voice, *a Santa Rosa, California-based publication providing news and commentaries on politics and culture. In the following viewpoint, Petersen questions the principle of self-determination with regard to the issue of Tibet's struggle for sovereignty. Petersen contends that the issue of self-determination for Tibet is not sacrosanct and cannot be considered in isolation from its impact on the lives of other Chinese.*

Kim Petersen, "The Tibet Question: Is Self-Determination, as a Principle, Absolute?" *Dissident Voice*, April 29, 2008. Reproduced by permission of www.dissidentvoice.org.

As you read, consider the following questions:

1. In Petersen's view, what is the state of workers' rights, wages, and conditions of employment in China? How do the struggles of Tibetans differ from those of most working Chinese?

2. In the author's opinion, what jeopardizes Chinese security?

3. According to the author, what type of freedom will people be permitted in an ideal world?

In Tibet, there appear two main streams within the Tibetan resistance to Chinese domination. One stream, led by the Dalai Lama, claims to be friendly to China and desires only greater autonomy—not independence. Another stream calls for Tibetan independence. Since progressivism is guided by morally derived principles, how does this approach bode for the people of Tibet's aspirations for self-determination?

Many progressives, human rights advocates, and opportunistic right-wing ideologues point to the principle of self-determination. In the United Nations [UN] Charter, Article 1(2) states:

> The Purposes of the United Nations are:
>
> To develop friendly relations among nations based on respect for the principle of equal rights and self-determination of peoples, and to take other appropriate measures to strengthen universal peace . . . .

This principle, as enounced in the UN Charter, leads many people to call for the independence of Tibet. They point to the principle of self-determination as if it were a sacrosanct, inviolable concept. But is the principle of self-determination an absolute? As a guiding concept, self-determination is fine, but as an absolute, inviolable principle, self-determination is flawed.

For example, do the resource rich regions of Bolivia have a right to separate from the rest of the state and horde the wealth? Is this what self-determination is about? Given that the Bolivians in the provinces of Santa Cruz, Beni, Pando and Tarija are predominantly of European derivation, it would be akin to according preeminent territorial rights to the descendants of colonialists. Is this what self-determination is about?

As a second example, the predominantly French-speaking province of Québec has long flirted with separation from federation with Canada. However, since the sentiment for separation varies by geographical region within Québec, anti-separatists propose a partitioning of the province should separatism ever carry the day in a referendum. Moreover, thoroughly undermining the self-determination aspirations of Québécois (mainly Francophones) is that it is based on the rejection of the self-determination of the Original Peoples of Québec! Is this what self-determination is about?

China and Tibet

I have never been to Tibet, but I lived one year in China. China is ruled by a Communist Party dictatorship. It is certainly no longer a dictatorship of the proletariat. Workers' rights, wages, and conditions of employment are abysmal. The situation is far from optimal, but some people argue that the Chinese are better off than previously.

Just as Tibetans struggle, so do the bulk of China's citizens. It is the plight of villagers and most working Chinese. Granted, the struggles differ. The Tibetan struggle is mainly for sovereignty, whereas the daily struggle for most Chinese is primarily economic. Tibetan self-determination, however, might impact upon all of these people. This presents a quandary: Can the Tibet Question be legitimately considered in isolation from its impact upon other Chinese?

It must be affirmed that while the right to self-determination might not be sacrosanct, the human rights of

Tibetans are inviolable. The Chinese regime must be pressured to uphold human rights, and it must be held to account for violations of human rights. The human rights of Tibetans must be respected, absolutely. . . .

Tibetan self-determination is predicated on factors such as history, culture, religion, distinctiveness, resistance to outside oppression, and desire to chart its own path. Tibetans do have a history—a long history. But does a long history, whatever that history may be, accord a preeminent right to self-determination? The long history also reveals that, aside from expanding its territorial realm, Tibet has been under foreign suzerainty for many centuries, including British, Chinese, and Mongolian. Is there a statute of limitations on aspirations for self-determination? If self-determination is a principle based in morality, then one would argue against such a limitation.

Universality of Self-Determination

If Tibetan aspirations for self-determination are still valid after many centuries, one wonders about other regions where self-determination has, much more recently, been suppressed and rejected. Quickly, the Zionist annexation and occupation of historical Palestine springs to mind. Zionist Jews point to "their" Israelite ancestors, Yahweh's promise, and a 3,000 year history to mask and excuse the undeniable racism toward the indigenous Palestinian people. . . .

Elementary morality decrees that whatever condition you seek to impose upon another being, you must, first and foremost, also impose upon yourself. All nations and all peoples must be accorded equality of rights. If the western world wants to criticize China for suppressing a Tibetan independence/greater autonomy movement, then it must not be guilty of shutting its eyes to the Palestinian struggle to regain their historical land. But it is even worse than a willful blindness to the plight of Palestinians because the western world is

China's Policy on Tibet

Critics of China say that it should allow Tibet to have autonomy, to preserve its traditional culture and to allow the Dalai Lama to return to Tibet.

China says that Tibet has long been part of China, that Tibet has benefited from modernization, and that the Dalai Lama should not be allowed to return because he aims to split Tibet from China.

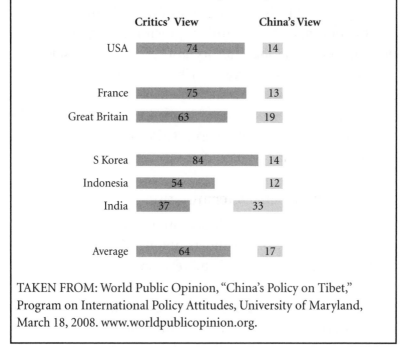

	Critics' View	China's View
USA	74	14
France	75	13
Great Britain	63	19
S Korea	84	14
Indonesia	54	12
India	37	33
Average	64	17

TAKEN FROM: World Public Opinion, "China's Policy on Tibet," Program on International Policy Attitudes, University of Maryland, March 18, 2008. www.worldpublicopinion.org.

complicit in the colonization, forced transfer, and genociding of the people in historical Palestine.

The cases of western complicity in gainsaying the sovereignty of other peoples are, regrettably, myriad. In recent times, there is the British-American expulsion of the people of the Chagos Archipelago [a group of islands in the Indian Ocean], ruled illegal by the British High Court in 2000. The ruling has since been subverted by two Orders-in-Council preventing the Chagossians from returning home.

The "national interests" of Britain and the US [United States] have, obviously, taken precedence over the rights of the Chagossians.

This abrogation of law harkens back to the "war criminal" president Andrew Jackson. Jackson had spearheaded the Indian Removal Act, a genocidal transfer program to displace the Original Peoples, leaving the land for the colonialists to settle. The Cherokee (Tsalagi) opposed Jackson. In a landmark 1832 decision, chief justice John Marshall of the U.S. Supreme Court ruled in favor of the Cherokee in *Worcester v. Georgia*. The Cherokee Nation was ruled sovereign and protected from removal laws. Jackson, in a flippant affront to the law of the US, dismissed Marshall's ruling: "He has made his law. Now let him enforce it."

The countries of the western hemisphere, by and large, represent an affront to the principle of self-determination. Therefore, if western states, and the citizens of those states, wish to condemn China's sovereignty over Tibet, then for such criticism to be valid, it must be applied in equal measure to the sovereignty of the US, Canada, Mexico, and to the other countries on down to Tierra del Fuego. Canada and the US exist as colonial states forged on the blood-spilling, destruction, and theft of the territory of people who have lived in Turtle Island [Native American term for North America] since time immemorial.

Indeed, at this point in history, the US and Britain (abetted by other states) are murderously occupying Iraq and Afghanistan. What is occupation, if not the denial of the self-determination aspirations of the occupied peoples?

Other countries of the western world fare little better in their respect for the principle of self-determination. Aotearoa (New Zealand) and Australia were forged from the theft of the territory of Aborigines and Maoris respectively. Elsewhere in the South Pacific, France clings to New Caledonia, Tahiti, and Wallis and Futuna. The US clings to Guam, Northern Marianas ... Without turning to Britain, Africa, and the Caribbean, the point should be abundantly clear: Western states are in violation of the principle of self-determination, so they are in no unbesmirched position to criticize other violators.

Does this exculpate China from censure from other states that do not violate the self-determination of its peoples? To the extent that these states refrain from criticizing the US, Canada, France, Britain, etc., it would be highly hypocritical.

Let's suppose that there was a bellwether of states that were pure on the principle of self-determination for their own people and peoples abroad. Would that grant them legitimacy in denouncing Chinese dominion over Tibet? Yes. The same logic also applies to people who uniformly criticize all crimes of state.

Does this mean that China's stance vis-à-vis Tibet is weakened? No.

Tibet's Strategic Military Importance to the Defense of China

For China to relinquish Tibet would be to relinquish a key militarily geo-strategic position at the top of the world. The US has China militarily encircled. The US, through the CIA, has been funding the separatism in Tibet. Nonetheless, it is quite understandable that Tibetans aspiring to greater autonomy/independence have accepted such money.

Oneness is a core traditional embodiment of the Chinese consciousness. The return of Hong Kong and Macau were epochal events for Chinese nationalists, who still pine for the return of Taiwan to the Chinese fold. To lose Tibet, or Xinjiang, would be utterly unacceptable for the Chinese people who lost face during the years of unequal treaties and colonial occupation. Loss of face, however, is not an acceptable reason for continuing to occupy another people's territory.

The state of Israel constantly, and risibly, cites security concerns to justify its occupation of historical Palestine. But in the case of China, security concerns appear legitimate. Are the territorial integrity and security concerns of 1.3 billion Chinese of lesser importance than the desire for self-determination among 6 million Tibetans?

The Chinese know they are encircled. Many know of China's not-so-long-ago history of having lost face to foreign invaders. Many know of their battles with western imperialism. Many know that when Mikhail Gorbachev lost control of the USSR [Union of Soviet Socialist Republics] due to the economic pressures of confronting the West, the USSR fell apart leaving Russia surrounded by former-USSR satellite states. Unfettered western capitalism then precipitated the implosion of the once proud Russia, which was forced to fight to preserve its own unity, as separatists battled for independence in Chechnya. Many Chinese know the ages old axiom of "divide and conquer." Many, also, know that NATO [North Atlantic Treaty Organization] encroached into the states formerly behind the Iron Curtain, further humiliating Russia.

What, then, would Beijing expect to happen if Tibet is loosened from China? How long before separatism would strengthen in appeal to so-inclined Uighurs in Xinjiang? What would the separation of the already autonomous Tibet augur for a mainland reunification with Taiwan? How long would it be before a US military base is perched upon the Tibetan plateau?

The US has been vociferous about the appearance of another military presence in what it claims to be its sphere of influence. Did the US quietly demur to the USSR in stationing nuclear weapons in Cuba? Yet US nuclear weapons were once stationed near China—in Japan and South Korea.

Given the hypocrisy that many world states face on the principle of self-determination, one might criticize the Dalai Lama. How can the Dalai Lama court colonialist entities to support greater autonomy for Tibet? Does this undermine the legitimacy of a movement for Tibetan autonomy/independence?

Since the US is an undeniable proponent of colonialism, militarism, torture, genocide, and economic plunder abroad, and since, as already argued, the US stands guilty of far worse crimes against its Original Peoples (including stealing their territories), its imperialistic machinations in Asia must be seriously evaluated when critically contemplating China's incorporation of Tibet.

Human rights advocates and supporters of Tibetan self-determination stand on moral quicksand if they fail to accord equivalent rights to all marginalized, expelled, and/or genocided peoples. I submit that if human rights groups want credibility, they ought to focus on the greater evils. It is US imperialism that jeopardizes Chinese security. It is the US that has surrounded China. It is the US which was deeply involved in the political and territorial separation of Taiwan from the mainland.

When US imperialism falls, other imperialisms may well fall, too. There will appear an opening for peoples previously living under the cloud of imperialist intent. Human rights groups and supporters of self-determination for Tibet should target the removal of the military threat to China to achieve the conditions favorable for greater autonomy/independence in Tibet.

A moral paradox exists under the present China-Tibet scenario: One people's freedom must not be predicated on the denial of another people's freedom. . . .

The Tyranny of Statism

Ideologically, I am opposed to statism. Borders are a form of tyranny. Borders delineate property in the name of the state. Borders divide humanity.

In an ideal world, people will be permitted freedom of movement. Human decency will demand that visitors and newcomers must be respectful of the indigenous and legitimately long-settled peoples in a region. Erasing borders should facilitate an end to geo-political conflicts and wars over human demarcations. Furthermore, people must share the resources and bounty of the world. This would go a long way to eliminating classism, racism, poverty, and famine. This would be the revolution. The solution is simple. Finding the massive will and courage to implement the solution is the *sine qua non*.

The Tibet Question is a straw dog. Acceding to Tibetan self-determination—a principle fraught with dangerous potentialities—does not take into account, sufficiently, the legitimate security concerns of one-fifth of the world's population. . . . How long before neoliberalism subverts any trends to social justice in an independent Tibet? How long before US military bases and CIA listening posts are perched on the rooftop of the world?

Human Rights Are an Absolute

The state of China must be held accountable for its actions . . . but not in a human rights vacuum! Progressives, people of conscience, and human rights advocates must firmly support human rights for all peoples. China is a violator of human rights. It is not alone in this regard. Advocacy of human rights demands the denunciation of human rights violations everywhere with measures against the human rights abusers commensurate to the level of human rights violations.

Self-determination is not an absolutist principle. The rights of humanity as a whole are preeminent.

Periodical Bibliography

The following articles have been selected to supplement the diverse views presented in this chapter.

Amanda Bower	"Dalai Lama: Tibet Wants Autonomy, Not Independence," *Time Magazine*, April 16, 2006.
China Daily	"What Is the Dalai Lama's 'Middle Way?'" July 26, 2006. www.chinadaily.com.
The Dallas Morning News	"China Crushes Tibet, Again," March 21, 2008. www.dallasnews.com.
Lodi G. Gyari	"Testimony of Lodi G. Gyari, Special Envoy of H.H. the Dalai Lama at House Foreign Affairs Committee Hearing on Status of Tibet Negotiations," U.S. House of Representatives, March 13, 2007.
H.D.S. Greenway	"China's Grip on Tibet," *The Boston Globe*, October 23, 2007.
The Hindu	"The Question of Tibet," March 26, 2008.
Maura Moynihan	"Afraid of the Dalai Lama; China's Chance to Turn Toward Dialogue on Tibet," *The Washington Post*, October 18, 2007.
Zha Wang	"Exposing Dalai Lama as a Dishonest Person," *Beijing Review*, no. 16, April 17, 2008. www.beijingreview.com.
Mark Winwood	"Tibet: The Angst of Autonomy," *Tashi Delak!*, April 30, 2006. http://mwinwood.blogspot.com.
Carl Ying	"The Problem with 'Free Tibet,'" *Emory Wheel*, March 27, 2008. www.emorywheel.com.
Zang Yanping	"'Democracy,' Deceptive Garment of Dalai Lama," *China Daily*, November 14, 2007. www.chinadaily.com.

Will Tibet's Cultural and Ethnic Diversity Survive Chinese Rule?

Chapter Preface

There is no question that the rule of the Chinese Communist Party in Tibet and the cultural influence of the ethnic Han Chinese, together with financial subsidies, the rapid pace of modernization, and the packaging of Tibet to court the tourist dollar, have brought dramatic changes to the Tibetan plateau and to the lifestyle of its indigenous people. According to some, this change was long overdue and necessary for the health and well-being of the Tibetan people.

"Since taking control of Tibet, China has abolished the Indian-based caste system and agricultural serfdom. It has built medical centers, schools, roads, railways and airports, introduced telecommunications and cell phones, increased tourism and raised living standards. China believes in doing what is necessary to integrate Tibet into the 21st-century world," writes Lee Kaun Yew in a 2008 article in *Forbes* magazine.

India's national newspaper, *The Hindu*, contends, "Tibet itself is on an economic roll: It has sustained an annual growth rate of more than 12 percent over the past six years and is now on a 13–14 percent growth trajectory."

Critics with the Tibetan advocacy and human rights group, the International Campaign for Tibet, contend that "China's fast track economic policies in Tibet, based on a political agenda, are directly linked to the repression of the Tibetan people. They are the most serious modern threat to the survival of Tibet's unique religious, cultural and linguistic identity."

Since it assumed power in 1959, the Chinese government has acted to maximize the economic potential of Tibet, exploiting its resources and natural beauty. Reports show that tourism revenue is expected to exceed $700 million by 2010, and the number of visitors is expected to increase to 10 million by 2020. But the rapid influx of ethnic Chinese into Tibet, particularly to the capital city of Lhasa, according to critics, dilutes Tibet's distinct cultural identity and flaunts its traditional values. In addition, critics contend, Indigenous Tibetans do not benefit equally from the economic growth. Many of the new employment opportunities are open only to applicants who speak Chinese, and modernization schemes, critics contend, primarily serve the Han newcomers at the expense of the Tibetan environment.

Chinese government restrictions on the practice of Tibetan cultural and religious life continue to fuel dissent. As a part of China's ongoing "Strike Hard" Campaign, launched in 1996, monks and nuns are compelled to attend "patriotic re-education" sessions, and images of the Dalai Lama are forbidden. Monks and nuns who resist have been expelled from monasteries and nunneries. According to the advocacy group Students for a Free Tibet, "By the late 1990s, hundreds of monks and nuns were imprisoned throughout Tibet for taking part in nonviolent demonstrations for Tibetan freedom."

The Minorities at Risk (MAR) report, a project of the University of Maryland, contends, "China has increased its political and military control of the Himalayan region. Special army units, in addition to regular Chinese forces, are now in place in Tibet and work teams have been stationed in key monasteries. The number of political prisoners in custody has steadily risen."

Kalon Tempa Tsering, speaking for the Department of Information and International Relations (DIIR) of the Central Tibetan Administration, argues that the Tibetan people must have "sufficient political freedom to ensure the continued survival and integrity of a unique civilization." The Chinese government, on the other hand, asserts that religious freedom of the Tibetan people is "respected and protected in conformity with the law."

In the following chapter, various authors present their views on the issue of how Tibet's cultural and ethnic diversity has been impacted by close to a half century of Chinese rule.

"*Tibetans are slowly marginalized ... Tibetan food, Tibetan furniture, Tibetan costumes are all made by Han people now.*"

Tibet's Cultural and Ethnic Diversity is Threatened by Chinese Central Government

Lindsey Hilsum

Lindsey Hilsum is a writer for the British newspaper New Statesman *and a China correspondent for Channel 4 news. In the following viewpoint, Hilsum contends that China's modernizing of Tibet is a daily reminder to indigenous Tibetans of the disrespect of the Han Chinese who claim cultural superiority over them. The Han Chinese even go as far as to produce Tibetan goods for profit. Hilsum argues that the Chinese can control the Tibetans economically, but they will never be able to control them religiously or spiritually.*

As you read, consider the following questions:

1. According to Buddhists, how far back does the annual Yoghurt Festival date?

2. Why does the economic development of Tibet threaten Tibetan culture, according to the viewpoint?

3. Why are Tibetans cautious about talking politics to foreigners, according to the viewpoint?

Smoke from incense burners scented the air as crowds of pilgrims laboured uphill in the dark. At dawn, four monks in maroon and saffron robes climbed on to the roof of the Drepung monastery overlooking Lhasa. They blew deep, reverberating horns, heralding the moment when some 50 monks and pilgrims would emerge bearing a rolled-up, 35-metre-square thangka—a painting of the Buddha on cloth—and start their slow trek to the hillside where it would be unfurled.

Buddhists say the annual Yoghurt Festival dates back to the 11th century. After the thangka is spread, the faithful give monks and nuns yoghurt as thanks for weeks spent in meditative retreat. A few hours later, in one of the Tibetan capital's less lovely suburbs, the Yoghurt Festival Real Estate Show conjured a rather different atmosphere. It opened with speeches, ticker tape and the unveiling of key messages in Chinese, Tibetan and English: "The value of the modern villas are very large in Tibet," read one. Young Han Chinese couples browsed leaflets and rickety scale models of proposed high-rise apartment blocks. "Rise abruptly, new area Dragon Spring," read one advertisement.

Tibetan Culture in Chinese Control

Traditional Tibetans may be as devoutly Buddhist as ever, but modern China worships Mammon [material wealth]. More than half a century after the Chinese invasion of Tibet, and 48 years after the Dalai Lama fled into exile in India, China's Communist rulers are hoping that an economic boom will help them consolidate control over the recalcitrant region. Last year, 2.5 million tourists and business people—some westerners, but most Han Chinese—visited Lhasa. Now the new railway from Beijing has reached the Tibetan capital, the number is expected to increase by 80 percent this year alone. "It works on the principle of the market economy," says He Ben Yun, a smooth-talking, statistic-spouting official who serves as deputy director of the Tibetan Development and Reform Commission. Born in Hunan Province—"like Chairman Mao"—he has embraced China's post-Mao economic philosophy with enthusiasm. "More people mean more consumption. I think it's good. Nowhere can develop in isolation," he says.

According to government figures, Tibet's economy has grown by more than 12 percent per year for the past five years. In its attempt to deter "splittists"—those who believe Tibet should be independent—the government is trying to knit the Tibetan economy into the fabric of China. Chinese companies are encouraged to "go west" to start mines, tourism companies and other businesses, while Chinese provinces sponsor development aid and town twinning projects. The Hong Kong-based Information Centre for Human Rights and Democracy says more than 50 ethnic Tibetan officials have recently been sidelined, while a further 850 reliable Communist cadres from across China have been offered incentives to join others spending three years in Tibet.

At midday in the main square, in front of the Dalai Lama's traditional seat, the red and white Potala Palace, a skinny Chinese girl in evening dress was miming Chinese pop songs for an audience of imported officials and military officers. To show that this was part of the Yoghurt Festival, a huge cardboard cut-out of what looked like a cup of shaving cream had been propped up on one side of the stage. The officials in the audience sported baseball caps from Amway, an American "multilevel marketing" company. They took pictures with their mobile phones, while police kept the public well back.

It's a common complaint that only the Han and other migrants, such as the Muslim Hui, are benefiting from the boom. "They take up a big part of the employment market. They settle and start their families here. Tibetans are slowly marginalised," says Woeser, a Tibetan dissident writer who was expelled from her government work unit in Lhasa for praising the Dalai Lama. (Like many Tibetans she uses just one name.) "They not only build houses and open restaurants in Tibet, but they're also taking over the traditional Tibetan industries. Tibetan food, Tibetan furniture, Tibetan costumes are all made by Han people now," she said. Such views are taboo in Tibet. Woeser's blogs have been blocked and her book, *Tibetan Journal*, banned. She now lives in Beijing, but still travels around provinces with Tibetan communities to gather information. When she visits her family in Lhasa, she is closely watched.

Tibet is more solidly under Chinese control than ever before, yet the government remains nervous of dissenting views. While Beijing-based foreign journalists travel without supervision in most of China, the government imposes a "minder" on all correspondents visiting Tibet officially. When asked why, Mr. He says it is because of the high altitude. "Our main concern is that journalists should adapt physically," he says. Journalists who try to work after entering as tourists are frequently harassed or arrested.

Government Resettlement of Tibetans

Tibetans are cautious about talking politics to foreigners, but—although there are still political prisoners—these days the Chinese attitude tends to be more patronising than brutal. It is official policy to tolerate ethnic minorities and their religions, provided they are loyal to the party and the state. "The government pays full respect to ethnic customs," says Mr. He. "Tibetan culture is an exotic flower among Chinese cultures. It has existed for more than 2,000 years. But we will help them remove bad or backward habits, and lead them to a more civilised life." As part of its civilising mission, and to integrate Tibetans into the modern economy, the government

Obliteration of the Tibetan Identity

Abuses of Tibetans' human rights—civil, political, social, economic, and cultural rights—are under an assault unlike any in the past decade. . . .

Tibetans have continued to tell Human Rights Watch about abuses for speaking out against Chinese political repression or attempts to practice their religion. Now they speak about the slow obliteration of their very identity—their livelihoods, their right to choose where they live, their ability to be educated in their languages—and the stark choices they face: to remain in Tibetan areas under these constraints, or to flee to other countries.

Sophie Richardson, "No Capitulating to China,"
La Libre Belgique, *May 14, 2007. www.humanrightswatch.org.*

has resettled 25,000 nomadic and farming families into "new socialist villages." The plan is to settle 80 percent of rural Tibetans in the next five years.

The countryside is being transformed, with small enclaves of white houses, many flying the red flag, along the roads. An hour's drive north of Lhasa, 260 families have been resettled in the village of Sangbasa. The railway runs past the new houses, each guarded by a ferocious, chained dog. There is no doubt that these houses are an improvement on the huts and tents in which nomadic herders used to stay, nor that settlements make it easier for older people to get medical help and children to go to school. Huang Qian Min, a half-Han half-Tibetan official, explained that it should be possible for Tibetans to continue their traditions while living in improved conditions. "They can live in the settlements in winter and herd animals in summer. Then they can go on herding and enjoy the modern life at the same time," she said. Asked whether the programme was designed so the party can control Tibetans better, she said such an idea was ridiculous. "When they were scattered, they knew very little about the world. Through TV and radio, they become more knowledgeable and make more progress. By living together, they can exchange ideas and improve themselves," she said. TV and radio are controlled by the Chinese government; only those with access to the Internet or shortwave can hear alternative views.

Suo Nang Zhuo Ma's grandchildren were herding yaks in front of her new house, which boasted glass windows and a comfortable sofa, as well as a television. At 58, she looked 20 years older, and appeared to have little nostalgia for the harsh life she had led, tending livestock and bringing up six children. "With help from the Communist Party of China, we have started a happier life, without many worries," she said. But those who have had to give up the nomadic life altogether are struggling. The train runs over the Tanggula Pass to Qinghai Province, which has a substantial Tibetan minority.

Concerned that overgrazing is damaging the fragile grasslands, the government has instructed several thousand Tibetan nomads to sell their herds and move to newly built suburbs on the outskirts of Golmud, a bleak mining town.

The result is ghettos—more than a hundred years on, the process of deprivation and deracination experienced by Aborigines in Australia and Native Americans in the US is being repeated high on the Tibetan plateau. Young men play pool at tables laid out along the street, or kick a ball around the dusty wasteland. Each family is given a house and the equivalent of £70 a month in welfare. "In the beginning, the Tibetan nomads are excited that the government is giving them free money to live in the cities, so they sign up to move, looking forward to living like the people they see on TV," says Woeser. "At first, they have money from selling their animals plus money given by the government, but over time, their money is used up. They learn to spend money like city people but they don't have the skills to make money like city people."

The Power of Religion

Most of the former herders are enthusiastic about education, but frequently Tibetan children—who may have never been to school before—are in classes of younger children, learning in Mandarin, which is not their native language. They face discrimination, often being seen as backward or stupid. Outside school, they have little interaction with non-Tibetan children, and are rapidly becoming an underclass.

While the men start to drink, the women increasingly turn to religion. One afternoon in mid-August, dozens of Tibetans, mostly women dressed in traditional clothes, packed into a small room in a Qinghai town to hear a visiting lama. For more than four hours, they spun their prayer-wheels and chanted, as children scurried in and out. On a table at the front, carefully concealed behind Coke bottles, biscuits and a vase of plastic flowers, was a portrait of the Dalai Lama. Showing such images is banned, because the Chinese government demands that its citizens be loyal only to the party. Yet some children sported medallions bearing the Dalai Lama's image and a 25-year-old former herder had created a shrine in his house, including a photo of one of his relatives posing with the Dalai Lama in Dharamsala, where the Tibetan government-in-exile has its headquarters. "The Dalai Lama is not only a religious, but also a national leader," says Woeser. "His international influence makes Tibetans proud. They like to prove that they're not like the Communist propaganda, which says they're backward and dirty."

Jealous of the power of religion, the Chinese government announced in August that lamas must have official permission to reincarnate—a directive which may prove a little hard to implement. The real target is the Dalai Lama, who is now 72. The Chinese hope that when he dies, all thoughts of independence will die with him, but they fear a repetition of the furore over the reincarnation of the second most holy figure in Tibetan Buddhism, the Panchen Lama. When the 10th Panchen Lama died in 1989, the Chinese government not only dictated who should succeed him, but "disappeared" the boy identified by the Dalai Lama as the true reincarnation. He is still missing.

In early August, Runggye Adak, an ethnic Tibetan, leapt on stage at an annual horse festival in Sichuan and shouted that the Dalai Lama should return, the imprisoned Panchen Lama should be released and Tibet should have independence. He is now in Chinese custody. At this summer's horse fairs, thousands of Tibetans eschewed their traditional ceremonial fur garments after the Dalai Lama said killing animals for fur was bad. The government allegedly threatened to penalise civil servants who did not wear fur to the festivals, seeing it as an indication that they were following the Dalai Lama.

As the sun rose above Lhasa, shafts of light fell across the grassy hill where a grid had been placed so the giant Yoghurt Festival thangka could be spread. As Sakyamuni, the Buddha, was slowly revealed, a great sigh of joy rose from the crowd. Monks and pilgrims threw white silk scarves known as hadas on to the image in a gesture of reverence.

The momentum towards modernity in Tibet is unstoppable. Physically, the Chinese Communist Party can dictate where people live and how they are governed. It can bring in millions of tourists and business people. But, after half a century, it still cannot control what Tibetans believe.

> "The new western railroad ... will transform Tibet from a thinly populated nation with a largely nomadic population and exotic, remote tourist destinations into a more common and accessible place. For many Tibetans, especially adaptable youth, opportunities will multiply ..."

Tibet's Cultural and Ethnic Diversity is Not Threatened by Chinese Central Government

John Makin

John Makin is a writer for The American. *In the following viewpoint, Makin asserts that the Lamaist State of Tibet is already a memory and that Tibet should focus on the future. Makin discusses the construction of the Beijing-to-Lhasa railway and how it benefits Tibet in a multitude of ways, such as bringing tourists to Tibet. He believes that China has increased opportunities for Tibetans and that they can now look forward to a better future because of the Chinese government.*

John Makin, "The Lhasa Frontier," *The American*, January/February, 2007. Copyright 2007 American Enterprise Institute for Public Policy Research. Reproduced with permission of *The American Enterprise*, a national magazine of Politics, Business, and Culture (TAEmag.com).

As you read, consider the following questions:

1. How much did the People's Republic of China spend building the railroad from Beijing-to-Lhasa?

2. According to the viewpoint, of what is the railway a symbol?

3. What is one way the railway benefits Tibet, according to the viewpoint?

In 2005, Americans spent about $10 billion on women's intimate apparel—fancy underwear, if you like. That's consumption in its most extreme form. Meanwhile, between 2001 and 2006, the People's Republic of China spent $4 billion building a 710-mile rail line to connect the western Chinese city of Golmud and Tibet's ancient capital, Lhasa. The new connection completes a 2,525-mile route across China that is no less important than the rail link between the east and west coasts of the United States, finished in 1869 when the "golden spike" was hammered at Promontory Summit, Utah.

China Invests in Tibet via a Brand-New Railway

But the new Tibet rail line is a symbol, not of similarity between the United States and China, but of contrast. It highlights the difference today between the richest country in the world and the country that is gaining wealth at the fastest pace. One is consuming, the other investing.

I traveled to China in June to see the giant construction project firsthand and to judge its economic significance—which I found to be considerable and unambiguous. For all its size and importance, the Tibet rail line has received little serious attention in the American media—in part because the Chinese themselves have been relatively quiet about it. They see no reason to stir up more controversy among American critics, like the movie actor Richard Gere, who decry the destruction of the Lamaist culture over more than a half-century of Communist rule.

When Tibet was incorporated into the PRC [People's Republic of China] in 1951, a rail link became a necessity. At the time, the western outpost of the Chinese railroad was Xining, 1,200 miles from Lhasa. The new Communist regime, for tactical military reasons alone, needed to move large quantities of troops and supplies westward in order to defend its remote regions against incursions from either Mongolia in the north or India and Nepal in the south.

The first portion of the line extension—from Xining to Golmud—was not completed until 1979, with regular service beginning in 1984. Golmud is still essentially a military outpost, but it is acquiring a wider economic base as China drives to develop its vast western region. Golmud now has major natural gas extraction and shipping facilities, and Israeli firms have been hired to enhance irrigation and farming in the desert that surrounds the city.

It was not until 2000 that China's former president Jiang Zemin ordered completion of the link from Golmud across the Tibetan border to Lhasa—a route that climbed the formidable Tanggula Pass, which, at 16,640 feet, is the highest railway elevation in the world.

The main alternative to the railroad has been a narrow, crowded, and dangerous two-lane highway, littered with the carcasses of abandoned vehicles. Driving up to the Tanggula Pass to get a close look at the rail line itself, I was reminded of the main reason that Tibet is so isolated. Most of the region lies on a plateau nearly 14,000 feet above sea level where breathing is difficult and Diamox pills are essential to avoiding severe bouts of altitude sickness. Our party, gasping for breath as we drove through a June snow flurry on the way to the pass, had no difficulty imagining the discomfort experienced by potential invaders of Tibet. Any move toward Lhasa or one of the few other cities of the region would require movement over long stretches of arid, oxygen-deprived, stormy territory.

The Beijing-to-Lhasa Railway Benefits Tibet

Tibet, for better or worse, has been a region waiting for a train—the ideal vehicle to connect it with the rest of the world, militarily and commercially. Air travel is a distressing alternative. The best way to deal with altitude sickness is to ascend slowly and to rest below the day's highest point. But travelers who fly into Lhasa make an abrupt entry at high altitude—12,000 feet above sea level—and hotel lobbies in the city look like hospitals, with half of the guests carrying oxygen tanks. To make matters worse, the major tourist attraction in Lhasa is the Dalai Lama's Potala Palace, where a visit entails a difficult and sharp climb from the square below.

The train addresses Lhasa's altitude problems because it moves gradually to Tanggula from Golmud and then proceeds nearly 5,000 feet down the other side of the mountains to Lhasa. Our party found the air in Lhasa more than adequate after the privations of the pass.

Meanwhile, trucks and buses traveling between Golmud and Lhasa not only ply a dangerous route but also are limited, because of the narrow road, in the freight and passengers they can carry.

The rail is opening Tibet to business. On August 30, two months after the railroad opened, William Mellor of Bloomberg News wrote that "shares in listed companies that do business in Tibet have climbed as much as 300 percent in anticipation of new markets, cheaper freight rates, and increased tourist numbers. . . ."

> The new western railroad creates a bittersweet reality. It will transform Tibet from a thinly populated nation with a largely nomadic population and exotic, remote tourist destinations into a more common and accessible place.

Tibet's Unique Spiritual Technologies

While other societies put their physical and mental resources into conquest, industrialism, and physical science, Tibet put hers into spiritual exploration. The result was that although Tibet remained materially backward well into the twentieth century, she had developed spiritual "technologies" well beyond anything accomplished anywhere else. While Europe was busily sailing caravels across the oceans, conquering the world, Tibet set out on a much more important and difficult exploration, that of inner space. . . .

Tibetan culture survives with some vigour in the diaspora and much of it is now available to non-Tibetans in translation and through direct teaching. It may be that this cultural spread is a silver lining to the tragedy of the Chinese conquest. . . .

I can envisage one scenario that might yet save Tibet, although it is a long-shot. It may yet happen that the cultural spread of Tibetan Buddhism may wash over into China itself, infecting the youth of that land with ideas of harmlessness, contentment and transcendence. . . .

China is now in a phase of deep spiritual winter. But human beings need spiritual sustenance. The religious void in China cannot last forever, something will have to fill it.

Ajahn Punnadhammo, "Bhikkhu's Blog-Tibet,"
March 22, 2008. http://bhikkhublog.blogspot.com.

One of the most popular of these companies is the grandly named Tibet Galaxy Science & Technology Development Co., a diversified firm based in Lhasa that is engaged in both beer production and medical treatment of brain tumors using radiation. Beer accounts for three-quarters of revenues, and the company has a joint venture with Carlsberg International called Lhasa Brewery that distributes beer (slogan: "The Beer on the Top of the World") mainly in the Tibet Autonomous Region. Shares, which trade on the Shenzhen exchange, tripled in the year ending June 2006 in anticipation of the railroad's opening, then dropped by about one third by the end of October. Tibetan stocks are not for the faint-hearted.

The Chinese Central Government Has Contributed to Tibet's Economic Growth

Tourist travel to Lhasa has already risen by 50 percent since 2004, and by 2020, Tibet expects 10 million tourists annually (or about four times the current level of the country's entire population). Tourists are expected to account for about 18 percent of the region's GDP [gross domestic product].

Even if it does not include the full costs of land acquisition and labor (since troops were used), the price tag of $4 billion that the PRC places on the building of the railroad seems ludicrously low for such a difficult engineering project with such a huge potential payoff. Over one half of the line must traverse fragile and unstable permafrost, which can turn to mud in the summer months, undermining the bed of a normal railroad. As a result, tracks are carried above the ground, over a network of bridges and causeways. This produces an odd sight: the rail line, at its higher elevations, appears to be built over some natural obstacle, like a river, but none is present.

The 48-hour journey from Beijing to Lhasa is made in fairly Spartan conditions. A hard seat for the full route costs about $50, and a sleeper berth between $100 and $150. Several investors, both Chinese and foreign, already have plans to operate private tourist trains along the tracks, and my impression was that the appeal for upscale tourists, taking a luxury train across the entire width of China and ending in relative comfort in Lhasa, will be immense.

Just as important as bringing passengers to Tibet is that the new railroad will bring freight—7.5 million tons a year, or about three tons for each of Tibet's 2.8 million residents. (By comparison, U.S. railroads in 2005 carried about six tons per capita.) Tibet's sparse population is spread over a region the size of France, Germany, and the UK combined, and the annual per-capita income is just $1,000, about one-seventh the level in Shanghai on the east coast. It is no wonder that China is trying to develop and populate its less prosperous western area.

With its many rivers and mountain gorges, Tibet will be a valuable source of electric power for the rest of China, and the region has significant deposits of copper, gold, and other minerals that will now be far easier to obtain and move to market. Western companies will undoubtedly participate in building hydropower facilities and extracting mineral wealth. And they have already benefited from the construction of the rail line itself. General Electric supplied the 78 custom-built 3,800-horsepower locomotives, at a cost of about $150 million. For $181 million, Canada's Bombardier provided the 361 sealed cars with oxygen facilities and special protection from Tibet's powerful sunlight and nasty thunderstorms.

While there's concern that the economic benefits of Tibet's development—like its hydroelectric power—will flow east, the truth is that the railroad is a classic case of a public good whose benefits to the broad Chinese population far outweigh those that could be expropriated by a private producer of the line. The externalities, in the jargon of economists, are substantial and positive. Construction of the railroad could only be completed by the Chinese government—both because of thorny right-of-way issues and because of the substantial risks involved in developing the technology to build a rail line at such high altitudes over permafrost. China is moving toward great-nation status at a remarkably rapid pace, and part of that process includes making huge capital investments to integrate its disparate regions, including Tibet, into a coherent nation.

The Chinese Government Enhances the Future of Tibet

The extraordinary technological challenges to building a rail line from scratch in Tibet are considerably easier to overcome, especially for a powerful centralized regime like China's, than the legal and political challenges to improving a key rail connection (like Boston—Washington) in the world's most advanced economy. Also, at this point in history, the Chinese clearly value public infrastructure more than Americans.

The new western railroad creates a bittersweet reality. It will transform Tibet from a thinly populated nation with a largely nomadic population and exotic, remote tourist destinations into a more common and accessible place. For many Tibetans, especially adaptable youth, opportunities will multiply; the loss of a unique history will seem less troublesome to them than it is to the isolated, older population.

The Lamaist State of Tibet is already a memory. Chinese soldiers invaded in 1950, and Tibet became part of the PRC a year later. After an unsuccessful rebellion, the Dalai Lama went into exile in India in 1959, and it is clear that the Chinese will not tolerate the re-emergence of a theocracy—especially since the government has endowed the west with so much strategic importance. In 1979, Deng Xiaoping declared that China should get on with development. "I don't care," Deng said, "whether the cat is black or white, as long as it can catch mice."

Whether Tibetans will fare better under the Chinese government than they did under the Lamaist theocracy remains to be seen. The outlook for traditionalists is bleak, but for most Tibetans, the chances for a better future are enhanced by the construction of the rail line to Lhasa.

> *"Today, Tibetans stand at an economic threshold, about to be overwhelmed by the tsunami of China's great expansion in ways that may ultimately be more devastating than the previous decades of repressive rule."*

Chinese Tourism, Migration, and Modernization Threaten Tibet's Unique Culture

Abrahm Lustgarten

Abrahm Lustgarten is a widely published, award-winning photo-journalist and investigative reporter. He is author of the upcoming book China's Great Train: Beijing's Drive West and the Campaign to Remake Tibet. *In the following viewpoint, Lustgarten argues that Tibet's culture has been packaged for tourism. He contends that the migrant Han Chinese now dominate all sectors of the economy, leaving out the Tibetan people due to the unfair rules in a new economic world.*

As you read, consider the following questions:

1. In Lustgarten's opinion, what was the focus of the 2008 mayhem in Lhasa, Tibet, that began as a protest by monks? Who joined the monks in the streets?

Abrahm Lustgarten, "What They're Really Fighting for in Tibet," *The Washington Post*, March 23, 2008, p. B03. Reproduced by permission of the author.

2. What group, according to the author, makes up the majority of the increase in Tibet's population and benefits most from the economic expansion?

3. In the author's opinion, how might the 2008 Beijing Olympics be of benefit to the Tibetan people?

On a winter night not long ago, I walked through the glowing doorway of Lhasa's newest nightclub, Babila, for an interview with its owner, a Chinese entrepreneur. Disco balls spun from the ceiling. Fiber-optic strands of plastic beads drizzled down like rain to a long, sleek stainless steel bar. On the stage, dancers in stiletto heels and lingerie gyrated to thumping music.

"Tibetan culture is so deeply rooted here," the owner told me. "I don't think it will be diluted—it's important for business." Yet looking around, I saw no Tibetan employees, and Tibetans represented only a smattering of customers. The bar served mostly Chinese businessmen and army officers, whose tabs could run as high as $2,000, several times the per capita income in Tibet.

The nightclub owner's comments underscored the problem Tibetans have with Chinese rule. Their culture has been packaged for tourism. Business is booming. But they aren't getting any of the bounty.

This, more than violations of human rights and religious freedom, is what fueled the riots in Lhasa and across Tibetan areas that started on March 14 [2008]—the largest and most violent protests since an uprising in 1959, when Tibetans rebelled against Chinese rule. Today, Tibetans stand at an economic threshold, about to be overwhelmed by the tsunami of China's great expansion in ways that may ultimately be more devastating than the previous decades of repressive rule.

It is certainly true that human rights abuses continue in Tibet, including imprisonment and torture, the banishment of Tibetans from their farmland, and draconian restrictions on activities and thought within the monasteries. And it is these restrictions that may have sparked this latest resistance. But the mayhem in Lhasa was most notable for its focus on the symptoms of the economic shift. What began as a protest by a few hundred monks from Lhasa's monasteries turned into a riot that brought shopkeepers, traders and farmers into the streets.

The targets of destruction and violence were not random. The cars toppled and burning in front of the Jokhang Temple, the 7th-century holy site at the heart of Lhasa's old city, and on the nearby Beijing East Road were expensive Toyota Land Cruisers and slick Hondas and Audis. They represent the upper class of Tibet's bureaucratic society and the ruling Han immigrants from China. The shops burning were Chinese-owned stalls and businesses, many of which were built since Beijing renewed its push to bring intensive development and encourage Han migration to the Tibet Autonomous Region in the late 1990s.

Chinese Dominator of Tibetan Economy

Six years ago, on my first visit, Lhasa could still be described as a quaint city brimming with Chinese influence but largely characterized by its ancient Tibetan architecture, Tibetan goods and, of course, Tibetan people. The Chinese who did reside there often left in the winter, when temperatures drop below freezing and the 12,000-foot-high city is whipped with winds off the Himalayan plateau.

I was dumbfounded, on four subsequent visits, to see how much had changed. The population exploded—from 250,000 to 500,000—and despite official figures that insisted otherwise, few of the newcomers were Tibetan. And they stayed in Lhasa year-round.

The Chinese had taken sledgehammers to large swaths of Lhasa's historic streets—narrow cobblestone alleys pinned in by 400-year-old whitewashed buildings. They replaced entire

An Insignificant Minority Within Their Own Homeland

Today we watch China as it rapidly moves forward. Economic liberalization has led to wealth, modernization and great power. I believe that today's economic success of both India and China, the two most populated nations with long histories of rich culture, is most deserving. With their new-found status, both of these two countries are poised to play important leading roles on the world stage. In order to fulfill this role, I believe it is vital for China to have transparency, rule of law, and freedom of information. Much of the world is waiting to see how China's concepts of "harmonious society" and "peaceful rise" would unfold. Today's China, being a state of many nationalities, a key factor here would be how it ensures the harmony and unity of its various peoples. For this, the equality and the rights of these nationalities to maintain their distinct identities are crucial.

With respect to my own homeland Tibet, today many people, both from inside and outside, feel deeply concerned about the consequences of the rapid changes taking place. Every year, the Chinese population inside Tibet is increasing at an alarming rate. And, if we are to judge by the example of the population of Lhasa, there is a real danger that the Tibetans will be reduced to an insignificant minority in their own homeland. This rapid increase in population is also posing serious threat to Tibet's fragile environment. Being the source of many of Asia's great rivers, any substantial disturbance in Tibet's ecology will impact the lives of hundreds of millions.

Tenzin Gyatso, the Dalai Lama,
"The Future of Tibet," delivered at the acceptance of the
U.S. Congressional Gold Medal, Washington, D.C., October 17, 2007.

neighborhoods with hastily built office buildings and dreary shops with all the hospitality of self-storage units. A $10 million shopping complex, its five stories bedecked in glass and billboards of scantily clad underwear models, opened blocks from the Jokhang. (The complex was torched in the protests.) Chinese dominated all sectors of the economy; they sold all the fruit, drove most of the taxis and mined all the minerals. And finally, in July 2006, the acclaimed Qinghai-Tibet railway opened for service, a transformation that released the floodgates.

In the accepted Western narrative on Tibet, economic development itself is villainized, the suggestion being that Tibet should remain as it was a thousand years ago because it represents something so peaceful and idyllic. Poor, yes, but how picturesque. It feeds the simplistic cliche of Buddha-loving pacifists oppressed by the atheist Chinese. The assumption is that Tibetans feel this way, too.

Left Out and Losing Faith

But in interviews with Tibetans, I heard a different thread: Many had been eager for modernization and had anticipated its perks—higher living standards, more education and better jobs. At first, they had welcomed the promised price drops and opportunity the railway was supposed to bring. But as the perks failed to materialize, they lost faith in a system that seemed blatantly designed to leave them out.

On a cold winter night in the capital, a young Tibetan entrepreneur gave me his perspective. "This is the universal trend," he said, gesturing to the thriving rows of lit storefronts and bustling commerce around us. "It would be happening whether China was doing it or Tibetans were doing it."

This man was trilingual, educated at one of Beijing's best universities. But he was having trouble making it in the new economy, and he was not alone. Another Tibetan man complained that he'd lost his guiding license after police began to enforce rules requiring annual exams—in Mandarin. Another reported that police forced him to rename his business after a Chinese investor chose the same name for his own shop. Meanwhile, signs for Tibetan businesses had universally been translated into Chinese, with small, scarcely visible Tibetan subscript as an afterthought. Tibetan identity was being chiseled away, replaced by the pell-mell flow of new businesses, new initiatives and new laws to support them.

In October 2006, several hundred young educated and otherwise "modern" Tibetans gathered in front of the local government administrative offices in Lhasa in what may come to be viewed as the precursor to the widespread unrest of March 14 [2008]. The protesters didn't take aim at religious persecution or human rights complaints but at the unfair rules of their new economic world. They were upset that, despite their own education and middle-class standing, jobs were going to Han Chinese instead.

The Chinese portray all that has happened in Tibet as progress, attributing the whopping 12 to 15 percent growth in gross domestic product in recent years to an almost philanthropic commitment to Tibetan culture. But their policies seem to have been aimed at something quite different.

The Olympics Are an Opportunity for Attention

China has consistently pursued a policy of "taming" its far-flung western regions through economic and ethnic assimilation. It has crafted tax incentives to encourage Han business owners to move west from eastern cities and has loosened migration rules. "Go West, Young Han" is the clarion call of the times. Chinese state-run firms have staffed large construction projects such as the railway and even local road building with Han Chinese contractors and crews, who send their earnings home.

All the expansion and wealth that has streamed into Tibet has benefited Tibetans very little. Even after decades of investment, the illiteracy rate remains four times that of neighboring Sichuan province, and there are one-fourth fewer vocational schools per capita than in the rest of China.

The Beijing Olympics in August [2008] afford Tibetans—and many other downtrodden Chinese—what may be their last great opportunity to draw the world's attention to the inequity of China's economic miracle. For the Tibetans, it may be their final chance to hold onto an ethnically, religiously, and economically unique homeland before it is lost forever. This is what makes the uprising of 2008 different from that of 1989, and this is what is bringing Tibetans into the streets.

Back at that nightclub in Lhasa, I asked the young owner whether he thought that the rising inequality was worrisome. His sanguine response nodded to the Chinese policy of seeking stability in Tibet by flooding it with Chinese: "It is very Han-friendly," he said. "There are many Sichuanese people now, [so] I feel more comfortable."

"With an enlightened programme of environmental protection, and with scrupulous respect for the language, culture, religious beliefs and constitutionally mandated autonomy of the Tibetan people, rising China is eminently capable of achieving the all-round development of this autonomous region."

Chinese Tourism, Migration, and Modernization Do Not Threaten Tibet's Unique Culture

Narasimhan Ram

Narasimhan Ram is an award-winning journalist and editor in chief of The Hindu, *India's national newspaper, and of other publications. In the following viewpoint, Ram argues that the economy of the Tibet Autonomous Region (TAR) is a benefit to the Tibetan people and that China's modernization of the region has brought material prosperity that is visible in villages, farming communities, schools and medical centers, and in the fast-developing transportation, telecommunications, and energy infrastructure.*

Narasimhan Ram, "Tibet in the Time of High Economic Growth," *The Hindu*, July 3, 2007. Reproduced by permission.

As you read, consider the following questions:

1. According to the author, by how much did Tibet's economy grow in 2006? How much food grain was produced in the region?

2. How much carbon dioxide is absorbed by Tibet's Lhalu Wetland annually?

3. What is acquiring "cult status around the world"?

Starting from age-old isolation from the mainstream, a chequered history, a low economic base, and a unique plateau environment averaging higher than 4000 metres in altitude, Tibet—the Tibet Autonomous Region (TAR), to give it its proper name—is on a roll. [In 2006] its economy grew by 13.2 percent compared with 10.5 percent for China as a whole. Its GDP [Gross Domestic Product] climbed to a level of 29 billion yuan, approximately $4 billion (still a tiny part of China's $2.68 trillion GDP). With foodgrain production touching 920,000 tonnes, the region was able to feed all of its people. According to Nima Tsiren, a confident Tibetan who is vice-chairman of the regional government, TAR's fiscal revenue grew by 14 percent over 2006, which enabled about 8 percent of the increase to be distributed. The per capita annual net income of its townspeople was 8900 yuan (compared with 6448 yuan in 2000), and of its farmers and herdsmen 2435 yuan (compared with 1331 yuan in 2000).

The arrival of material prosperity, steady population growth, rises in living standards, education and skills training, and in general, the process of modernisation are transforming life, work, and mindsets, especially of the young who make up the bulk of the Tibetan population. . . .

The effects of the transformation are conspicuous on Lhasa roads and streets, with their fast-moving vehicular traffic and rising modern buildings and commercial complexes. They can be witnessed on Barkor Street, known locally as 'the Saint Road,' and in the crowded bazaar around Jokhang Temple; in the vicinity of the Dalai Lama's long-vacant Potala Palace; in the fast-developing transportation, telecommunications, and energy infrastructure; and at another high altitude wonder, the 6.2 square kilometer Lhalu Wetland in the capital's suburbs, which is reckoned annually to absorb 78,800 tonnes of carbon dioxide and produce 53,700 tonnes of oxygen. The results are on view in surrounding villages, especially in the households of farmers who have prospered thanks to their hard work and thrift, the large number of working hands in the family, central government subsidies, and new opportunities offered by the construction boom. The positive effects are visible in the schools, kindergartens, and medical centres dispensing Tibetan medicine, which is acquiring cult status round the world. They are also on view in the bustling, grain-producing and industrialising Xigaze prefecture located in TAR's mid-south. . . .

Economic Benefits

During the first ten months of the operation of the Qinghai-Tibet railway, TAR saw its foreign trade rise by 75 percent—to $322 million. The trains have brought an influx of tourists, more than 2.5 million domestic and foreign tourists last year; and the number is expected to rise to 3 million this year. Taking the train to mysterious Tibet is becoming something of a national aspiration and it is affordable. Investment is likely to follow tourism and trade. Chinese officials project that by 2010 the Qinghai-Tibet railway will transport 75 percent of the autonomous region's inbound cargo, tremendously lower transportation costs, and double the tourist revenue. As they see it, the railway symbolises 'the right of Tibetans to seek development,' catch up with the rest of rising China, and open themselves more to the outside world.

Over the next decade, the railway will be extended to three more lines in Tibet, one connecting Lhasa with Nyingchi to the east, another with Xigaze in the west, and the third linking

"An Idealized Land of Goodness and Purity"

"Tibet, Tibet!" With those two words (well, one word repeated) Bjork caused a storm of controversy at her concert in Shanghai [in March, 2008]. The Icelandic warbler has joined a long list of celebrities, commentators and sportsmen who plan to use the platform provided by the Beijing Olympics to protest against China's occupation of Tibet. . . .

Pro-Tibet campaigners seem always to be outraged by two things in particular: China's incessant modernisation of Tibet, and its refusal to allow the Dalai Lama to return and assume his "rightful" position as Tibet's leader. . . .

Tibet has long been the plaything of people disillusioned by the modern world. Since James Hilton wrote *Lost Horizon* in 1933, in which Tibet was depicted as "Shangrila", Tibet has been used and abused, turned into an idealised land of goodness and purity by aristocratic and artistic elements in the west who despise the pace of change over here, and like the idea of a completely natural, archaic, mystical, politics-free land "over there." . . .

Too much of today's pro-Tibet campaigning is underpinned by two things: self-loathing for our own, apparently over-modernised societies, and a semi-colonialist view of Tibetans as spiritual children and the Chinese as evil automatons.

Brendan O'Neill, "The Problem with Tibet,"
March 6, 2008. www.guardian.co.uk.

Xigaze with Yadong on the China-India border. A luxury tourist train offering five-star comfort, like India's 'Palace on Wheels,' is in the works. . . .

Apprehensions about the railway's adverse effects on the environment and wildlife have proved exaggerated if not wholly baseless. . . .

Aside from the railway, the development of a new kind of physical infrastructure—highways, paved roads, bridges, power lines, telecommunications, irrigation channels, modern housing, and so forth—is there for all to see. The plan target is to build, by 2010, 'high-class highways' to connect 100 percent of Tibet's townships and 80 percent of its administrative villages; and to convert 80 percent of the roads into blacktops. Expressways, however, are considered unsuitable for a region that has only 2.3 persons per square kilometres.

Old and New

As you speed along the highway from Lhasa to Xigaze for five hours or more, you are offered rapid frame alternations of the new and the old, the modern and the traditional, in a heady mixture of sensory experiences. A surprise is how easily you can connect to the outside world: the GPRS [General Packet Radio Service] on your mobile phone (or PDA) works along much of the Lhasa-Xigaze highway. While browsing the Internet for news of the outside world or answering your e-mail, you can catch a glimpse of how the bulk of Tibetans live: in mud and stone houses; cultivating small plots and tending livestock; prayer flags fluttering; primitive farming and nomadic practices; basic living conditions; colourful long skirts, striped aprons, beads, and incongruous cowboy hats; people squatting road-side; and little girls and boys in school uniforms on their way home.

That Tibet under the Dalai Lama-headed theocracy had no schools worth speaking about, and that the illiteracy rate was 95 percent, are indisputable facts. From such an abysmal base, it is hard not to make substantial progress. The Chinese socialist system showcases the "fast, coordinated, and healthy development of education" in TAR as a solid achievement of liberation and especially of the post-1979 reform. . . .

The development gap between town and country is certainly a matter for concern in Tibet—as in the rest of China and also in India—but a high level of central government subsidies and organised social sector assistance from China's more developed provinces and municipalities are targeted at narrowing the gap. China has adopted a strategy of westward development to overcome the historical backwardness of this vast part of the country.

With a speeding up of the development of industry, the service sector, infrastructure, and education; with the modernisation of agriculture and livestock practices; with adequate job creation; with an all-out poverty eradication effort; with an enlightened programme of environmental protection; and with scrupulous respect for the language, culture, religious beliefs and constitutionally mandated autonomy of the Tibetan people, rising China is eminently capable of achieving the all-round development of this autonomous region, which has been problematical in the past. Seldom does a giant country get such an opportunity to concentrate its burgeoning resources, internal and external, to improve the lives of 2.81 million of its citizens, accounting for 0.21 percent of the national population, dotted across 1.22 million square kilometres, actually one eighth of China's land area.

"It is odd that the atheistic Communist Party should give itself religious authority, including the right to decide when a reincarnation is valid or invalid, legal or illegal."

Chinese Rule Threatens Tibetan Buddhism

Frank Ching

Frank Ching is a Hong Kong-based journalist and commentator. He is author of several books including Ancestors: 900 Years in the Life of a Chinese Family *and the forthcoming* China. *In the following viewpoint, Ching argues that the new regulations governing Tibetan Buddhism are meant to ensure that the Chinese government will control Tibet's future religious leaders and will continue to extend its authority into Tibet's religious affairs.*

As you read, consider the following questions:

1. According to Ching, what stipulation in China's new regulations bars the Dalai Lama from the process of choosing the next living Buddha?

2. When was the title "living Buddha" first conferred on a Tibetan religious leader?

Frank Ching, "China Tightens Grip on Tibetan Buddhism," *The Japan Times*, August 23, 2007. Copyright 2007 The Japan Times Ltd. Reproduced by permission.

3. What is the state religion of the Chinese Communist Party, according to Ching?

China announced [in July 2007] new regulations governing Tibetan Buddhism, including a stipulation that senior monks, known as "living Buddhas," cannot be reincarnated without government permission.

"The reincarnation of living Buddhas must undergo application and approval procedures," the new regulations stipulate. Living Buddha reincarnations with a "particularly great impact," such as presumably of the next Dalai Lama, "shall be reported to the State Council for approval."

The new regulations, which come into effect September 1 [2007], were issued by the State Religious Affairs Bureau under the State Council, which implements religious policy set by the Communist Party. Its director, Ye Xlaowen, far from being a religious leader, is an alternate member of the Communist Party's Central Committee and hence, by definition, an atheist.

It is odd that the atheistic Communist Party should give itself religious authority, including the right to decide when a reincarnation is valid or invalid, legal or illegal.

Clearly, the new regulations are meant to ensure the Chinese government's control of future Tibetan religious leaders, in particular future Dalai Lamas. The current Dalai Lama is 72 years old and lives in exile in India, beyond Beijing's control. This is a situation that Beijing wants to change.

Beijing accuses the Dalai Lama of being a separatist who advocates Tibetan independence. Not surprisingly, therefore, an article in the new regulations declares: "Reincarnating living Buddhas should respect and protect the principles of the unification of the state."

It also stipulates that the process of choosing reincarnations of living Buddhas cannot be influenced by persons or

Regulations on Tibet's Religious Affairs

On January 1, 2007, the Chinese government put into effect the new "TAR Measures in Implementing the Regulations on Religious Affairs". Yet again the so-called order no. 5, a new and more vigorous regulation on reincarnation was put into effect from 1st of September 2007. Each and every article of the new regulations indicate a harder and a more aggressive approach in controlling the religious activities— from contents of the religious text and teaching to the general management activities within the religious communities. Such regulation has placed even repairing to the structure of the existing monastery under the state control. . . .

The general suggestion that there is more relaxation of religious freedom in the Tibetan areas outside TAR [the Tibet Autonomous Region] stands challenged as scores of arrests and detentions, and severe crackdowns were reported from those areas. . . .

Enforcement of such adverse religious policy is gradually reducing the value of the religious institutes to a mere spot of tourist attraction. Religious freedoms of the Buddhist Tibetans are intensely targeted to bring an enforced stability in Tibet.

Tibet Information Office,
"Half Yearly Review of Human Rights in Tibet,"
December 4, 2007.

organizations outside China. This means that the Dalai Lama, the highest spiritual leader of Tibetan Buddhism, is barred from the process.

No Reincarnations Outside China

However, Tibetan Buddhism teaches that certain individuals can consciously decide to be reborn in order to return to the world to help others. The new regulations mean that the Chinese government will not recognize reincarnations outside the country.

The Dalai Lama has said that if the present situation regarding Tibet remains unchanged—that is, a Tibet that does not enjoy true autonomy—he will choose to be reincarnated outside Tibet.

But even though the Dalai Lama has numerous supporters both in Tibet and overseas, his passing will be a great blow to the Tibetan cause. Even though his followers may designate a Tibetan boy born in exile as the new Dalai Lama, it will be many years before that person is in a position to exercise leadership and be influential internationally.

In the meantime, Beijing will use its own methods to choose the next Dalai Lama. And that boy will be brought up and tutored under the eye of the Chinese government. Meanwhile, many Tibetans in China will have little choice but to accept the officially designated successor.

The new regulations make official something that has been China's position for years. In 1995, for example, the Dalai Lama endorsed the designation of a boy in Tibet as the reincarnation of the last Panchen Lama [second highest ranking spiritual leader in Tibet] who had died in 1989. But the Chinese government picked a different boy and declared him the Panchen Lama's real reincarnation.

Beijing has defended its involvement in Tibetan religious affairs by citing precedents going back to the Yuan dynasty (1279–1368) of the Mongols and the Qing dynasty (1644–1911) of the Manchu. The title living Buddha was first conferred on a Tibetan religious leader in the 13th century by Kublai Khan, the Mongol leader who founded the Yuan dynasty.

But there is a difference. The Mongols, who governed China during the Yuan dynasty, made Lamaist Buddhism the official religion and hence had the greatest respect for Tibetan religious leaders. Similarly, during the Manchu (Qing) dynasty, the emperor was a patron of the Dalai Lama.

Atheism: A State Religion

While no doubt the religious activities of Mongol and Manchu rulers were to some extent a cloak for justifying their imperial ambitions, they did purport to uphold and revere the traditions and beliefs of their various subjects.

The situation today, however, is one in which the Communist Party, whose state religion is atheism, cannot be seen as either a believer in Buddhism or a patron of the faith. It is simply the state extending its authority into religious affairs.

This is similar to the current standoff between China and the Vatican, where Beijing insists on its right to appoint bishops. Ultimately, it all boils down to a matter of control. The Chinese government is unwilling to share power, even over religious matters.

On this point, a biblical injunction seems appropriate: "Render unto Caesar the things which are Caesar's, and unto God the things that are God's."

"All Buddhists should follow the tenets to distinguish right from wrong on cardinal issues and make further progress in their religious accomplishment. However, the 14th Dalai Lama has been playing with the divine Buddhism to achieve political goals and purposely mislead the public, which fully demonstrates his hypocrisy in faith."

The Exiled Dalai Lama Threatens Tibetan Buddhism

Shi Shan

Shi Shan is a reporter with the Xinhua News Agency, the official press agency of the People's Republic of China, and a research fellow in Tibetan Buddhism. In the following viewpoint, Shan argues that the Dalai Lama has violated the basic precepts of Buddhism that prohibit killing and lying. The author contends that the Dalai Lama stirred up unrest in Lhasa leading to loss of life and property, and that he violated the precept of no lying. In Shan's view, the Dalai Lama has used Buddhism to further his political goals.

Shi Shan, "Window of China: On the 14th Dalai Lama's Betrayal of Buddhism," October 11, 2007. www.chinaview.cn. Reproduced by permission.

As you read, consider the following questions:

1. According to the author, what are the four precepts of Tibetan Buddhism?

2. What are some of the ways, according to the author, that the Dalai Lama has broken the commandments and betrayed his faith?

3. According to the author, when the Dalai Lama fled abroad, how did he break the precept of no lying?

The basic criterion to distinguish pious Buddhists from bogus ones is "taking precepts as masters" and "abiding by precepts to practice Buddhadharma". Master Tsongkha-pa wrote in his book, the *Great Exposition on the Stages of the Path to Enlightenment*, that "the great achievers will be so only in name if they fail to fully follow Buddhist precepts and teachings." Though the commandments followed by Tibetan Buddhists vary, they are all based on the common ground of four precepts, namely no killing, stealing, adultery and lying. Monks would be seen as committing serious offenses if they betrayed one of the four precepts. However, the 14th Dalai Lama, a self-claimed "Buddhist leader", repeatedly broke the commandments and betrayed his faith by violating the precepts of no killing and lying.

Dalai Lama Stirred up Unrest

Firstly, let's look at how he betrayed the precept of no killing: In the late 1950s, Tibetan reactionary leaders launched an armed rebellion in an attempt to permanently maintain the feudal serfdom and their autocratic rule. The 14th Dalai Lama was the chief representative of the feudal serfdom. The armed rebels set houses on fire, looted Tibetan people, and raped women. What happened then still lingers in Tibetan people's minds today. In the late 1980s, the Dalai Lama clique stirred up unrest in Lhasa, which seriously harmed people's lives and damaged their property. Moreover, who was behind the mid-

1970s assassination of Gung-thang Tshul-khrims, one of the leaders of the Group 13, who failed to obey Dalai's orders? Who nodded to plot and implement the assassination of Li-thang A-thar? Who, in the late 1990s, sent killers to the home of Rin-po-che Kun-bde-gling and seriously wounded him? Who threatened to exterminate the "life and activities" of two young Rin-po-ches, Chi-jang and Sun-po? Vjigs-med Tshe-ring, who once was one of the key members of the Dalai Lama clique, said that at least ten Tibetans, who disagreed with the Dalai Lama, had been assassinated.

Secondly, let's have a look at how the 14th Dalai Lama violated the precept of no lying. The Dalai Lama sent a tele-gram in 1951 after the signing of the agreement on the peace-ful liberation of Tibet, in which he said that the agreement, signed on May 23, 1951, was based on friendship and thus won unanimous support from the local government of Tibet, Tibetan monks, and the people. But on March 10, 1961, the 14th Dalai Lama said in a speech that the agreement was writ-ten fully in the will of the "Red Han" and was signed by his representative, who was put under house arrest. In 1953, the 14th Dalai Lama wrote an article, saying that Tibetans were one of the ethnic communities in China, which enjoyed long and rich history and Tibetan people enjoyed freedom and equality as all the other ethnic groups did in China after they returned to the great family of the motherland. But on March 10, 1960, he said in another speech that Tibet has been "a completely independent country" with its own political system and government ever since the Tibetan people created their own written language.

Dalai Lama Defames Motherland

In 1954, I accompanied the 14th Dalai Lama and the 10th Panchen Lama to Beijing. Till now, the zealous and respectful manner that the Dalai Lama demonstrated during that visit is still vivid in my mind. In the eulogy he presented to Chair-

Dalai Lama Causes Deliberate Rift

Anyone without some knowledge of the history of Tibet or without studying the Dalai Lama's speeches over the past decades would possibly believe how much he has suffered unfair treatment, and how much he has harbored goodwill and sincerity in improving Han-Tibetan relations and worked for harmony between the two ethnic groups.

Now consider the recent violence in Lhasa, capital of Tibet, and regions beyond it.

It is not difficult to see that the beating, smashing, looting and burning by rioters were mainly targeted at either the Han or Hui ethnic groups.

The remarks that "Tibet has been integrated into the Han ethnic group," that "the fortune of Tibet has been plundered by the Han people," that "China has settled other ethnic groups to Tibet," that "the Chinese government has deliberately caused a rift in the Han and Tibetan people," and other such accusations that the Dalai Lama has spread are nothing but inflammatory lies aimed at causing ethnic friction.

Zha Wang, "Exposing Dalai Lama as a Dishonest Person,"
Beijing Review, *April 17, 2008. www.bjreview.com.cn.*

man Mao Zedong in both Tibetan and Chinese, he extolled Chairman Mao as the "red sun", which "glorifies the whole nation, drives away invaders, and brings peace and blessing to people of all ethnic groups". However, when he fled abroad, he went back on his words and broke the precept of no lying by wantonly attacking and defaming his home country and calling on the so-called free world to unite to block the development of his own people and motherland.

It is known to all that in the early Qing dynasty (1644-1911), the Fifth Dalai Lama paid respects to Emperor Shunzhi and was conferred by the Emperor with honorific title. The title and position of Dalai Lama was also legalized by the central authorities during the visit. The move not only helped maintain the unification of China, but also boosted the social stability and economic development in Tibet. The Tibetan people, who were profoundly grateful to the 5th Dalai Lama, commended him as "the Great Fifth". It was shocking to many people that as a descendent of the 5th Dalai Lama, the 14th Dalai Lama unabashedly attacked the 5th Dalai Lama in May 1986 at a gathering of Tibetan people in the Netherlands, saying that it was shameful for the 5th Dalai Lama to have "joyously accepted the mandarin jacket conferred by the Qing emperor." He also derided the 5th Dalai Lama for paying respects to the central authorities, saying he had "lost face by setting up the relations." Those sayings were Dalai Lama's real thoughts, which also proved that he had totally betrayed his ancestors and his religion.

The Dalai Lama Is Playing with "Divine Buddhism"

During the late 1980s and early 1990s, the 14th Dalai Lama believed that the dramatic changes in the former Soviet Union and eastern Europe brought new opportunities for "Tibet independence." In August 1991, he said in France and Switzerland that it would take no more than five or ten years for Tibet to be separated from China. In January 1992, he said again that Tibet would achieve independence in five or ten years. In 1995, it seemed that Dalai Lama gained more "magic power" even though his clique was low in morale. In March of the same year, he formally issued a prophecy, proclaiming that great changes would take place in China that year or in the following year. In August, he said in public that the "upcoming changes in 1995 or 1996" would benefit his group. As a matter of fact, Tibet did witness "great changes" in 1995. During that year, Tibetan people celebrated the 30th anniversary of the founding of the Tibet Autonomous Region, and most of the 62 key construction projects in Tibet financially supported by the whole nation were completed. Also in 1995, the divine reincarnation of Panchen Lama was successfully completed. The development of Tibet played a joke with the "magic power" of the 14th Dalai Lama, which, perhaps, is the judgment on Dalai Lama for his betrayal of the precept of no lying.

The spiritual essence of the tenets and canons of the Tibetan Buddhism include the basic essentials of observing the rules, sincerity, equilibrium, even share of wealth, altruism and harmony, which are also the basics of the healthy practice of Buddhism over the past 2,000 years and grounds for Buddhists to cultivate themselves through meditation and encourage people to do good. All Buddhists should follow the tenets to distinguish right from wrong on cardinal issues and make further progress in their religious accomplishment. However, the 14th Dalai Lama has been playing with the divine Buddhism to achieve political goals and purposely mislead the public, which fully demonstrates his hypocrisy in faith.

Periodical Bibliography

The following articles have been selected to supplement the diverse views presented in this chapter.

Frank Ching   "Rendering unto Dalai Lama What Is His," *The China Post*, August 22, 2007.

Tim Johnson   "Tibetans See 'Han Invasion' as Spurring Violence," March 28, 2008. www.mcclatchydc.com.

Joshua Michael Schrei   "A Lie Repeated: The Far Left's Flawed History of Tibet," *Dissident Voice*, April 5, 2008.

Robert Shepherd   "UNESCO and the Politics of Cultural Heritage in Tibet (United Nations Educational, Scientific and Cultural Organisation)," *Journal of Contemporary Asia*, May 1, 2006.

Ni Siyi   "Chinese Scholars Dismiss Dalai Lama's Concern Over 'Cultural Genocide' in Tibet," Xinhua (New China News Agency), Asia-Pacific Service, April 26, 2007.

Bhuchung K Tsering   "Tibetan Culture in the 21st Century," *Tibet Writes*, December 27, 2007. www.tibetwrites.org.

Chen Weijian   "Survival or Death of the Tibetan Race," *Epoch Times*, April 14, 2008.

Xinhua News Agency   "Reincarnation of Tibetan Living Buddha Must Follow the Rule of Law," China Tibet Information Center, December 26, 2007. http://eng.tibet.cn.

Liu Yandong   "Tibet's Development Has Broad Cultural Meaning," *China Daily*, October 17, 2006.

Lee Kuan Yew   "Two Images of China," *Forbes*, vol. 181, no. 12, June 16, 2008.

CHAPTER 3

Have the Tibetan People Benefited from Chinese Central Government?

Chapter Preface

The year 2008 was a particularly difficult time for China-Tibet relations. The rising dissent within Tibet from those feeling the brunt of religious and cultural restrictions on Buddhist practice was met with harsh and swift reprisals, according to some critics. Increasingly strident calls for independence have come from Tibetans in exile, and the passing of the Beijing Olympic torch through many countries has focused international scrutiny on the human rights of the Tibetan people and the survival of Tibetan culture. The devastation of the May 12, 2008, earthquake and its many aftershocks served to deflect the criticism of China for a time, especially when the Chinese government responded promptly and with unusual openness to the disaster. The epicenter of the 7.9 magnitude quake was Sichuan Province on the edge of the Tibetan plateau, an area with a large ethnic Tibetan population.

China's unwavering bottom line in any discussion on Tibet is the position that Tibet has been an inalienable part of China since the thirteenth century. Safeguarding national sovereignty and territorial integrity is of utmost importance to the Chinese Central Government, particularly since the so-called "peaceful liberation" of Tibet from what China characterizes as "savage and dark feudal serfdom."

Lindsey Hilsum, a China correspondent writing in the *New Statesman*, sees a different side to China's presence in Tibet. She argues, "As part of its 'civilising mission'—and to deter independence—China is taking control of the Tibetan economy. Modernity is being imposed by force, creating ghettos and spreading deprivation across the countryside. . . . More than half a century after the Chinese invasion of Tibet, and 48 years after the Dalai Lama fled into exile in India, China's Communist rulers are hoping that an economic boom will help them consolidate control over the recalcitrant region."

Eric Sommer, writing in an online commentary in the *China Daily* contends that "whatever the alleged grievances, and whatever we believe about Tibet, mobs armed with sticks, rocks, and firebombs cannot be allowed to rampage through the streets. . . . The Chinese government's restrained use of riot police to stop the recent violence in Tibet is not only fully justified; it is similar to, and far milder than, measures taken under similar circumstances by other governments."

Yan Zheng, a Tibetan specialist based in Sichuan Province, argues that since the Tibet Autonomous Region (TAR) was established on September 1, 1965, "Tibetans, under the leadership of the central government, have actively participated in the administration of national and local affairs, fully exercising the right of autonomy guaranteed by the Constitution and other laws."

According to Sophie Richardson, deputy director of the Asia Division of Human Rights Watch, however, "Tibetans from the Tibet Autonomous Region and other provinces with large Tibetan populations report with growing frequency the difficulty of finding schools that teach in their languages. Many are asked to pay up to $300 a year in school fees; this is often more than they make in a year. This situation is of course exacerbated by strict controls on admitting students to monasteries, which for years have been traditional sources of education. These realities prompt thousands of Tibetans each year to leave."

In the chapter that follows, various authors present their views on life in Tibet under the rule of the Chinese Central Government. The debate about whether the Tibetan people have benefited continues to be a source of ongoing tension. This is a clash of cultures and values between the spiritually grounded lifestyle of Tibetan Buddhism and the modernization imposed by the Chinese Central Government. Finding a just balance between competing interests will not be an easy task.

> "... They claim Tibetan culture is in-
> credibly wonderful. It is so wonderful,
> they say, that poverty and isolation are
> acceptable costs in the defense of this
> culture."

Tibetan Quality of Life Has Improved Under Chinese Rule

Kevin Z. Jiang

Kevin J. Jiang is a writer for the Harvard International Review. *In the following viewpoint, Jiang argues that the greatest threat facing Tibet is poverty. He says that China provides economic development, such as the construction of the Qinghai-Tibet railway line that will provide many opportunities for Tibet. Change, the viewpoint argues, is not always a negative thing, and he believes the Tibetan culture will survive and even become strengthened under Chinese rule.*

As you read, consider the following questions:

1. What are some of the arguments against the construction of the Qinghai-Tibet railway line, according to the viewpoint?

Kevin Z. Jiang, "Free Tibet . . . From Isolation," *Harvard International Review*, July 2, 2006. Copyright © 2006 The Harvard International Review. Reproduced by permission.

2. Why, according to the author, should we not fear a changing Tibetan culture?

3. How can Tibet help China, according to the viewpoint?

The story of Tibet took yet another turn yesterday with the official opening of the Qinghai-Tibet railway line in China, the first such connection between Tibet and the rest of China. The railway line is now the highest in the world; at one point, it reaches an elevation of 16,640 feet above sea level, over 3 miles high. To deal with the extreme conditions on the so-called "roof of the world," special technological adjustments were made, including elevating train tracks above the ground to deal with unstable permafrost and laying cooling pipes to further solidify the ground.

But like the other large Chinese construction/development project—the Three Gorges Dam—the railway is highly controversial. On one hand, the supporters claim that it will further open Tibet to the rest of China and help the region develop economically. Develop it must, for the standard of living in Tibet is far lower than that of the rest of the country, especially the booming cities on the east coast. Detractors, however, are deeply concerned about the potential impact on Tibetan culture as Han Chinese pour into the region. They also argue that whatever the benefits the railway might bring, they will only accrue to the new Han Chinese, not the Tibetans, whose poverty and lack of education will continue to inhibit their abilities to exploit any opportunities.

China's Economic Contributions Have Improved Tibet

The controversy over the Qinghai-Tibet railway line is really just a continuation over the debate over Tibet itself. A quote from a BBC News article neatly sums up the dilemma: "Tibet's extraordinary isolation has kept it poor. Education levels and

Bright New Houses Replace Smoky Hovels

Leaving aside the inequalities between Tibetans and migrant Han Chinese, there's no question that the Chinese have done a huge amount to improve the economic conditions of the indigenous population. Drive along the highway between Lhasa and Shigatse, seat of the disputed Panchen Lama, number two in the Tibetan Buddhist hierarchy, and you can see bright new houses being built to replace the smoky hovels many Tibetans used to occupy. True, part of this resettlement programme is aimed at settling nomadic herders whose mobility threatens China's grip. China recalls how nomads in eastern Tibet put up strong resistance following the invasion in 1950. But it would be a gross caricature to deny China's attempts to bring economic development to a disadvantaged region.

China says it has rehoused 10 percent of Tibet's population in 2006, building 279,000 new homes. Now that's progress. The high-tech, high-altitude railway, opened in 2006 and tying China more firmly to its Tibetan fiefdom, has brought a wave of new investment along with more migration. When I first visited Lhasa in 1993, people still defecated in the street. Now it is a modern and much bigger city, albeit a largely Chinese one.

Ed Douglas, "Comment & Debate:
Whatever China Does, Tibet Will Still Demand Its Freedom,"
The Observer, March 16, 2008, p. 35.
Copyright © 2008 Guardian Newspapers Limited.
Reproduced by permission of Guardian News Service, LTD.

life expectancy fall well behind the rest of China. But that isolation has also helped to preserve Tibet's unique culture and way of life."

So is the new railway line and opening of Tibet good for Tibetans? I strongly argue, yes. First, while critics are correct in pointing out that Han Chinese will reap most of the development, it does not address the fact that Tibetans are benefiting to a certain extent as well. Unfair, yes it is, that immigrant Han Chinese are the big winners (in the beginning at least). But economists and common sense would tell us that any gain is better than no gain, even if the other guys "unfairly" get a bigger share of the windfall. Indeed, the longer Tibet remains isolated, the more it will fall behind the rest of the world. The railway comes not a moment too soon.

But economics is dry, and the more interesting debate is about culture. I do not pretend that the railway will not affect the Tibetan culture in no way whatsoever. Already, parts of the capital Lhasa, with similar looking forgettable buildings and wide paved streets, look more like the generic modernized cities on the east coast than any other traditional Tibetan locale. This is an all-too-familiar story throughout the developing world. But before we become overly romantic and lament the loss of a beautiful past (a past that is poorer, nastier, more brutish, and shorter than we like to believe), we must think critically.

Assuming that Tibetan culture, like all other cultures, is not the perfect essence of Good, then it would not be completely rational to fear a changing Tibetan culture. What critics of the railway are defending is the status quo Tibetan culture. What they forget is the possibility that Tibetan culture can also change for the better. And if it is impossible to judge one culture better than another (as I believe), then it would be impossible to say that exposing Tibetan culture to incoming Han Chinese culture would be bad, for there is no good and bad here, only new and old.

The Chinese Central Government Will Help Tibetans Defeat Poverty

True, the Han Chinese culture has proven to be powerfully assimilative in the past. Mongols and Manchus successfully conquered China, but in the process became Chinese themselves. (Does anyone know a friend who speaks and writes Manchu?). But it is insulting to imply that Tibetan culture is so worthless that its existence cannot stand outside ideas and beliefs.

Those who are keen are protecting status quo Tibetan culture and who oppose the railway seem to have a contradiction in their own argument. On one hand, they claim that Tibetan culture is incredibly wonderful. It is so wonderful, they say, that poverty and isolation are acceptable costs in the defense of this culture. Yet, on the other hand, they argue vociferously that the increasing contact with the rest of China will threaten the very existence of this wonderful culture. If this culture is so fragile that it cannot survive contact with other civilizations, then is it really that wonderful? If the Tibetan people will flock so quickly to new Han Chinese way of life, then is it really so wonderful? And if it is so wonderful, will the Tibetans so readily abandon it?

Of course, many would argue and say that many wonderful cultures, from those of American Indians to native Africans to Australian aborigine, have suffered great losses. But in all those circumstances, the invading culture used force of arms to attack the native culture. The Communist party may be tough and biased masters in Tibet, but it is doubtful they will use force of arms to exterminate Tibetan culture.

Perhaps the most important thing to remember about the Qinghai-Tibet railway is that it runs both ways. At the same time that it will bring many Han Chinese to Tibet, it will also export greater knowledge of the region. We fear, loathe, and reject what we do not understand, and the railway will bring greater understanding of Tibetan culture to the rest of China. If Tibetan culture is as wonderful as its defenders, and I, believe it is to be, then we should all be confident that a greater opening up of Tibet will not only protect its way of life from ignorant bigotry, but also will make the rest of China a better place as well. It will teach the rest of China that there are

more important things to worship than Mammon and that simple goodness is still important, no matter how rich one is.

The story of Tibet took another turn yesterday with the opening of the Qinghai-Tibet railway line. Tibet took a turn for a better future.

> "More than half a century after the incorporation of Tibet into China, adequate and affordable health care is still not available to the majority of Tibetans."

Tibetan Quality of Life Has Deteriorated Under Chinese Rule

One H.E.A.R.T. (Health, Education and Research, Tibet)

One H.E.A.R.T. (Health, Education and Research, Tibet) is a not-for-profit group headquartered in Salt Lake City, UT. It operates in association with the University of Utah Health Services Center and in partnership with the Lhasa Prefecture Health Bureau in Tibet and the Center for Disease Control in Beijing, China. The organization acts to provide health care education and assistance to underserved Tibetan women and children through culturally sensitive training programs for rural health workers and community members that introduce life-saving child birthing skills to help women and children survive. In this viewpoint, the authors contend that adequate and affordable health care is still not available to most Tibetans after more than a half century of Chinese rule.

One H.E.A.R.T., "The Mission of One H.E.A.R.T. is to Save the Lives of Tibetan Women and Children, One Birth at a Time," April 8, 2008. www.onehearttibet.org. Reproduced by permission.

As you read, consider the following questions:

1. In the authors' view, why is it of "utmost urgency" to save the lives of Tibetan women and their children?

2. The authors contend that health and health care on the Tibetan Plateau are among the worst in China. Is there official data on morbidity and mortality on the Plateau?

3. In the authors' view, what has been the focus of Beijing's economic development policy for the western regions of China? What has been neglected?

Saving the lives of Tibetan women and their children is of utmost urgency for the survival of the Tibetan people and culture. Improving maternal health and reducing child mortality have globally been recognized as vital to promoting development and eradicating poverty, as set out in the United Nations Millennium Development Goals. . . .

Geography and Demographics

The Tibetan Plateau covers a total area of 2.5 million square kilometers; one fifth of the People's Republic of China (PRC). The Plateau is comparable in size to Western Europe. Tibetan-populated areas of China are administratively divided into the Tibetan Autonomous Region (TAR) on the one hand and Tibetan autonomous prefectures and counties in the Provinces of Gansu, Qinghai, Sichuan and Yunnan on the other. Each province is divided into prefectures. Each prefecture in turn is divided into counties, townships, and villages. A cluster of 10 to 15 villages or nomadic settlements forms a township. According to the 2000 census, the estimated population of Tibetans living in China is 5,416,021 people. Approximately, 45 percent of the Tibetan population is rural, while 40 percent is nomadic or semi-nomadic, and only about 15 percent live in urban areas. The harsh climate, an average altitude of 4,000 meters, inhospitable and rugged mountainous terrain, and lack of infrastructure in vast parts of the Plateau are all ad-

Tibetans at the Bottom

A new UN [United Nations] report that includes information on the quality of life of the Tibetan people indicates that Tibetans are virtually at the bottom of the economic and social ladder. In addition to being worse off than others in China, there is a growing disparity between Tibetans in rural areas and in urban areas. Some other information in the report also makes me feel that there is a new social division; between a group that is becoming the elite class, composed predominantly of officials, and the rest of the Tibetan society. . . .

The report shows that the regions in which Tibetans are located fall in the lowest eight ranks in the overall Human Development Index (HDI), with the TAR [Tibet Autonomous Region] being the 31st, which is the lowest rank, and Qinghai being the 27th. The HDI "is a comparative measure of poverty, literacy, education, life expectancy, childbirth, and other factors for countries worldwide."

Bhuchung K. Tsering, "A Look at Quality of Life in Tibet,"
Tibetan Review, *February 9, 2006.*

verse factors that have contributed to the isolation of the region, as well as particularly dire living conditions for the overwhelming majority of the population.

General Health and Health Care

Health and health care on the Tibetan Plateau are among the worst in China. In Tibet, there is a high incidence of diseases resulting from malnutrition and generally a serious lack of medical infrastructure, vital resources, and basic education in the health area. The central government, as well as international health organizations, often fail to report on the statistical disparities that exist between the wealthier and densely populated regions of Eastern China and the more underserved and scattered areas of Western China, including the Tibetan Plateau. No official data on morbidity and mortality exist for the Tibetan Plateau. According to some expert, the rate of maternal, child and infant mortality is so high that Tibet can be categorized as one of the least developed regions on earth. In addition to diarrhea, arthritis and pneumonia, they also report that the TAR has the highest rate of tuberculosis in China, and one of the highest incidences in the world of the rare Kashin-Beck (Big Bone) disease, which causes deformities and stunted growth. More than half a century after the incorporation of Tibet into China, adequate and affordable health care is still not available to the majority of Tibetans. Beijing's economic development policy for the Western regions of China, including the TAR, tends to focus on large-scale infrastructural projects, such as roads, railways, dams and power stations, while neglecting soft infrastructure, such as the provision of health care and education.

Maternal and Newborn Health on the Tibetan Plateau

The Tibetan society is one of the few in the world where a tradition of trained birth attendants does not exist. Poor nutrition, lack of trained health personnel, long travel distances, and limited access to emergency care place Tibetan women and infants at high risk of birth-related deaths. The vast majority of births take place at high altitude, in a cold environment and without access to electricity or health care. In spite of active campaigns by the Chinese Government to encourage women to give birth in a medical facility, more than 95 percent of Tibetan women give birth at home. Most babies are delivered with the help only of the mother or the mother-in-law whose sole assistance is the cutting of the cord. Amazingly, many Tibetan women deliver their babies completely on their own.

It is believed that Tibet has one of the highest newborn and infant mortality rates in the world. Tibetan women are three hundred times more likely to die than women in developed countries from various pregnancy and delivery complications. Postpartum hemorrhage is the leading cause of death. Likewise, babies are far more likely to die in Tibet than anywhere else in the world. Like in other cultures, a mother's death is devastating to her family for it often threatens the health of her children and impacts on the family for generations. The mother is the thread that holds the family together. When a mother dies, her surviving children are three to ten times more likely to die within two years. When a Tibetan mother dies, her surviving children are more likely to die young and less likely to attend school or complete their education. Also, many Tibetans believe that a mother's death during childbirth is a sign of bad spirits that brings misfortune to her family and community.

Improving maternal and child health is therefore essential to preserve the Tibetan people, their social fabric and cultural identity.

> "A standard system of education, in which school and university graduates can freely follow their family occupations or start a new occupation of their choice . . . will help prevent the situation of producing large flocks of unemployed graduates."

Tibetans in Exile Need Traditional Education

Tibetan Children's Educational & Welfare Fund

The Tibetan Children's Educational & Welfare Fund is a registered society of the Department of Education of the Central Tibetan Administration of His Holiness the Dalai Lama in Dharamsala, India. The organization functions to provide Tibetan students in exile with adequate care, an appropriate educational foundation, and the opportunity for higher study within the principles outlined in the Basic Education Policy for Tibetans in Exile. In this viewpoint, the authors contend that education is a lifelong process, consisting of both formal and informal learning. They argue that proficiency in the language and grammar of one's mother tongue is the gateway to any further learning.

Tibetan Children's Educational & Welfare Fund, "Basic Education Policy for Tibetans in Exile," www.tcewf.org, 2005. Reproduced by permission.

As you read, consider the following questions:

1. According to the authors, what is the ultimate goal of the Tibetan people? How would Tibetan education assist in meeting this goal?

2. The authors state two principal sources of traditional Tibetan education. What are these?

3. In the authors' view, what are the primary components of modern education?

A responsibility the Tibetan people have towards the world community is to preserve and promote the unique wealth of Tibetan culture and traditions, which are of great value to the whole of humanity, through all times and circumstances. Another responsibility the Tibetan people have to the world is to promote and widely propagate the noble principle of *Universal Responsibility* as introduced and initiated by His Holiness the XIV Dalai Lama. These responsibilities are to be fulfilled.

The ultimate goal of the Tibetan people is to transform the whole of the three *Cholkhas* [Regions] of Tibet into a zone of non-violence (*ahimsa*) and peace; to transform Tibetan society into a non-violent society; and to lead other peoples onto the path of non-violence and compassion. Thus, the Tibetan people must be made capable of correctly and fully understanding the direction, path and means to this goal.

Tibet is situated on the roof of the world and her wealth of natural resources has a close bearing on the well-being of all Asian nations and the world at large. Thus, it is of paramount importance that the Tibetan people should be able to preserve the natural environment of Tibet.

A political goal of the Tibetan people is to instill in all Tibetan races of the three *Cholkhas* the principles of unity, freedom, democracy, rule of law, non-violence, truth and justice. It must be ensured that all Tibetans irrespective of their age properly understand and live by these principles.

The Tibetan system of economy must also be in accordance with the aforesaid fundamental principles. The Tibetan people must therefore avoid: the two widespread extremes of capitalism and socialism; the two livelihood extremes of luxuriance and destitution; and reliance on *wrong means of livelihood*. A system ensuring self-sufficiency and right means of livelihood must therefore be followed.

Traditional Tibetan Education

The principal sources of the traditional Tibetan education are the traditions of *Yungdrung Bon* [native religion] and *Buddhadharma* [Buddha teaching]. Hence, *base, path* and *result*, and *view, practice* and *discipline* of the inner science contained in these traditions form the core of Tibetan traditional education.

The four other Tibetan sciences of Language, *Valid Cognition*, Art and Medicine together with their branches, which have been highly influenced by *Bon* and *Dharma*, are also subjects of traditional Tibetan learning.

The Tibetan Language, which is the medium of these traditional studies, despite its long period of development has undergone very few changes. It holds great potency to communicate intended meaning. It is a great store-house of many profound sciences and arts difficult to be found in other languages. It is, in fact, the only standard base of all Tibetan studies.

Modern Education

Modern education, unlike traditional Tibetan education, does not trace its origin to a religious or ancient cultural source. It, instead, is a system that was begun and developed in recent centuries by human beings through investigation and experimentation, primarily, on external objects and phenomena. It developed further and was spread more widely in the course of time.

Education in Exile

The first real step in the exile education movement took place on the cold and windy morning of March 3, 1960, a year after coming into exile. On that date, His Holiness the Dalai Lama formally opened the first Tibetan school in exile at Mussoorie. With an initial enrollment of 50 students, this modest beginning was to blossom in the years to come with the establishment of many new Tibetan schools in India, Nepal and Bhutan. By the end of the millennium, the number of Tibetan schools had grown exponentially to 106 kindergartens, 87 primary level, 44 middle level, 21 secondary level and 13 senior secondary level schools, with total enrollment of over 25,000 students.

More than 37,000 children have completed a moderate level of education over the years, many of whom had gone on to universities, medical and engineering colleges and vocational institutes in India and abroad. On completing their higher education, almost all have come back to serve the community as teachers, doctors, health workers, administrators, social workers, technicians, engineers etc.

Kalon Thupten Lungrig,
Tibetan Children's Educational & Welfare Fund,
April 11, 2008. www.sherig.org.

Modern education primarily includes the study of science and technology, mathematics, social sciences, economics, management and planning, and most arts subjects which fall under the category name of "science".

The Aim of Education

Students must be enabled to fully awaken their discriminative faculty of mind to be able to distinguish right from wrong.

This would empower them: to be confident to make decisions with freedom of thought and action; to be self-reliant in livelihood, i.e. to live without depending on or exploiting others thereby ensuring their freedom of livelihood by right means; and to be able to protect the freedom of the individual and community by non-violence thereby ensuring the freedom of security. This constitutes the principle of *"freedom"*.

By embracing other beings as more precious than the self and sacrificing the self for the service and welfare of other persons, the noble spirit of altruism is to be generated and established. This constitutes the principle of *"altruism"*.

For the sake of future generations, the environment and natural resources must be conserved for the peaceful sustenance of this planet, and people must be empowered to uphold their ancestral cultural heritage. This ability to preserve culture and environment constitutes the principle of *"upholding the heritage"*.

In relation to the general well-being of the world and in accordance with the needs of time and place, we must be able to introduce new principles, systems, objects, movements and so forth. This constitutes the principle of *"innovation"*.

Raising citizens to be endowed with these four stated qualities shall be the aim of giving education. . . .

Tibetan Language Is the Medium

In an education system having traditional education as its core, it is appropriate to have the medium in which the traditional learning abides as the medium of instruction for general education. Hence, efforts shall be made to gradually convert the medium of instruction in all Tibetan institutions of learning from the pre-primary level up to the highest research study level, into Tibetan language.

Inherent to traditional as well as modern learning is the content meaning and the vehicle that conveys it. As proficiency in the vehicle of speech is gained with the study of language and proficiency in content meaning is gained with the study of *Valid Cognition (pramana)*, the Tibetan language and *Valid Cognition* shall be taught with special emphasis at the basic school level.

In order to empower students to investigate and reflect on obscure phenomena and to develop confidence in presenting their findings after investigation before the world's scholars, the process of learning by *hearing* and *thinking* as indicated by *Tibetan Inner Science* shall be widely introduced and promoted.

In order to instill into pupils the principles of wholesome thought and conduct from the pre-primary school level, the quality and role of teachers, formation of school curriculum, and methodology of teaching shall be framed mainly in accordance with the traditional Tibetan principles and sciences, rather than the modern system.

A standard system of education, in which school and university graduates can freely follow their family occupations or start a new occupation of their choice, shall be introduced. This will help prevent the situation of producing large flocks of unemployed graduates.

> "In all the government run schools it is mandatory for the students to give their first priority to Chinese language starting from elementary school. . . . Those who fail to score good marks in Chinese are not eligible to apply for higher studies."

Tibetan Education Under Chinese Rule Is Inadequate

Tibetan Centre for Human Rights and Democracy (TCHRD), Dharamsala

The Tibetan Centre for Human Rights and Democracy (TCHRD) based in Dharamsala, North India, is a Tibetan human rights organization with the mission to promote and protect human rights of the Tibetan people in Tibet, and to educate the exile Tibetan community on human rights principles and democratic concepts. TCHRD is the first such nongovernmental organization to be established in exile in India. In this viewpoint, the authors contend that China's so called modernization of Tibet and the increased presence of military and Han Chinese in Tibet have resulted in few restrictions on prostitution. More Tibetan women

Tibetan Centre for Human Rights and Democracy (TCHRD), "Unfavourable Education Policies Compel Tibetan Girls into Prostitution," *Tibet Today*, vol. 1, January 10, 2007. Reproduced by permission.

without access to education and adequate employment are turning to prostitution for economic survival.

As you read, consider the following questions:

1. In this viewpoint, the authors quote a recent Tibetan exile, Namdrol Lhamo, who told of her experiences with the educational system in Tibet. In the authors' opinion, what was the chief reason why Namdrol was deprived of pursuing her higher studies?

2. In the authors' view, why are young Tibetan women from outside the capital city forced to earn their living with prostitution? What other jobs do they lack credentials to obtain?

3. Other than educational limitations, what other factors do the authors cite as being responsible for conditions the authors characterize as a decline of moral values in Tibetan society?

Lhasa, the capital city of Tibet, which was once a sacred Buddhist pilgrimage destination is rapidly turning into a haven for prostitution due to China's ongoing drive to develop and modernize the Tibetan region. The flesh trade is getting piled up in a sophisticated way eluding the curious eyes of the outside world. The so-called hair salons and bars during daytime turn into brothels at night. The age of women working in the flesh trades are mostly between 16 to 40 years, though some are even younger. Due to lack of education opportunities and professional skills, they opt for flesh trade hoping that the money would secure a better life in the future. The prostitutes consist of both Chinese and Tibetan women in the brothels, but Chinese are paid more than Tibetan prostitutes.

The reason for the rise of this trade can be attributed to China's modernization drive, presence of a large military contingent in Lhasa living without families, and development projects like the railway between Golmud and Lhasa which has brought in large number of Chinese settlers to Tibet.

A 12-year-old Namdrol Lhamo, who hails from Lhasa, feels that increasing number of Han Chinese in Tibet particularly in and around Lhasa city at such a high rate would bring many sociological changes, particularly the most alarming being the corrosion of ethical and traditional moral values of the Tibetan people.

First Priority to Chinese Language

Namdrol Lhamo, who recently arrived in exile, had the opportunity to study till 12th grade, but was unable to pursue higher studies, as she was unable to score the required marks by .5 percent. According to her, "in all the government run schools it is mandatory for the students to give their first priority to Chinese language starting from elementary school. If one is not fluent in Chinese language, it is very difficult to find a job even though one has passed the exam with good result. Those who fail to score good marks in Chinese are not eligible to apply for higher studies." That was the chief reason why Namdrol was deprived of pursuing her higher studies as she missed the requisite marks for Chinese language by a bare margin. Like her, many Tibetan youngsters in Tibet were deprived of taking their study further and consequently they ended up without any future. They would not be qualified for any decent job, thus, forcing them to take up some odd job in hotels, guest houses, restaurants, discotheques, bars and brothels as there are no other alternative sources of livelihood.

Namdrol, after failing in exam, took up a job at a hotel in Lhasa city and worked there for nearly four years. She said, "The owner of the hotel is a Tibetan and there are nearly 140 workers and most of them are Tibetans. Most of the employees have been to middle school and were forced to discontinue their higher education owing to lack of tuition fees as the schools charge exorbitant fees while there were some who

Constant and Vigorous Indoctrination

The current education policy of China is aimed at getting Tibetans to assimilate Communist ideology rather than to preserve Tibetan culture, tradition, language, religion and history. Tibetan children who have escaped to exile report receiving almost no education regarding their cultural heritage, but say they were constantly and vigorously indoctrinated into Chinese culture and communism. . . .

The enrollment and completion rates of school-age Tibetan children in primary school paint a grim picture. The enrollment rate of girls in Tibet is the lowest and dropout rate is fourth highest in the nation, the highest being Ningxia. . . . It is estimated that roughly 33 percent of all Tibetan children receive no education at all. This is a huge figure compared to the 1.5 percent of Chinese children who are illiterate. According to "Tibetan Center for Human Rights and Democracy's 2006 Annual Report," the education for Tibetans is overpriced, and under-funded. For example, the annual fees range from 20 to 6,000 yuan (US $3 to $750) per month. This is unaffordable for most Tibetans, especially those in rural areas, who earn an average of 800 yuan (US $100) per month.

An internal Tibet Autonomous Region (TAR) Party Committee document reveals that schools in the TAR are collecting as much as thirteen different kinds of fees from students, six of which are illegal. . . .

Tibetan Women's Association (TWA),
"Report by TWA to the United Nations' Human Rights Council,"
March 20, 2007. www.tibetanwomen.org.

can afford the fees but fail to qualify the requisite mark by 3 percent. The qualification required for getting an employment in restaurants, hotels, dance bars, travel agencies and clubs can be met if an applicant has a middle school degree and should have good command in Chinese language. The government set the criteria that those who do not know Chinese language will not get jobs in these sectors and anyone who applies for job has to give qualifying exam in Chinese language."

Wasted Lives and Income

Most of the workers in hotels were Tibetan girls and they were mainly from Lhasa city. Those Tibetan girls who came from Kham, Amdo and outside of Lhasa were not fortunate enough to get employed in hotel and restaurant, as they lack proficiency in Chinese language. Hence, left with no other alternatives, and thus indulge themselves in prostitution to earn their living. The number of such girls is increasing these days. For example, in Lhasa city many young Chinese and Tibetan girls engage in prostitution to earn their livelihood. Most of the brothels are owned by Chinese women and hence many Tibetan girls emulate the Chinese prostitutes and choose prostitution as an alternative way to eke out livelihood. Tibetan brothels are not conspicuous from outside, but have a Bodsod (literally: Made in Tibet) word inscribed on the doors and beer is served inside the room. There are many young Tibetan men who visit the brothels. Moreover, most of tour guides of the foreign tourists were frequent visitors to the brothels as they have more money than other Tibetans. They drink beer in brothels and afterwards they take the prostitutes to the hotels. These Tibetan youngsters waste their hard earned income in brothels.

It is being reported that the government doesn't levy any restriction on the sale of beer and the plying of the flesh trades as they pay heavy taxes to the government. That is the reason why brothels, nightclubs and dance bars function freely without any restriction from the government authorities. Hence, the number of brothels in Lhasa has been increasing rapidly over the years. The Tibetan girls working in brothels are in the age group of 16 to 40 years. The numbers of Tibetan girls working in brothels are increasing in Lhasa city these days. In light of this fact, the opening of railway link between China and Lhasa will only pave the way for massive influx of Chinese migrants to Lhasa and will subsequently increase the Chinese prostitutes in Tibet. Before the occupation of Tibet, one could hardly find any Tibetan prostitute in the town. Since the Chinese invasion, owing to the influx of Chinese settlers in Tibet, the prostitution business in Tibet particularly Lhasa city has experienced massive growth of the sex industry.

Declining Moral Values

This business in many ways corrodes the social life of the communities. Chinese settlers lure the elder Tibetans by paying huge money in exchange for young Tibetan girls. These elder Tibetan deceive the young Tibetan girls from rural areas and bring them to towns and cities to work as prostitutes. Due to the prevalence of prostitution, many family men tend to devote more time and money with prostitutes leading to breakdown in families. Namdrol Lhamo has witnessed many such cases while working at hotel in Shigatse prefecture.

In recent times, Lhasa and Shigatse authorities have imposed no restriction on prostitution in hotels and guesthouses. However, couples are required to show their marriage certificate while booking room for their stay in hotels.

No restriction is imposed by government on the functioning of brothels, bars, nightclubs and intakes of drugs and abuses. Namdrol Lhamo views that the massive increase of brothels, bars, and night clubs is due to the massive influx of Chinese settlers in Tibet and thus it leads to decline of moral values and decadence in general Tibetan society.

> *"China controls the flow of information in Tibet, tightly restricting all media and regulating Internet use. . . . In universities, professors cannot lecture on certain topics, and many must attend political indoctrination sessions."*

Tibet's Civil and Political Rights Are Abused by the Chinese Central Government

Freedom House

Freedom House is an independent nongovernmental organization founded in 1941 by Eleanor Roosevelt and other Americans concerned with threats to peace and democracy. Freedom House works with U.S. policy makers, governments of established democracies and international institutions. Through analysis, advocacy, and action, the organization acts to promote and preserve democratic values and to oppose tyranny. In this viewpoint, Freedom House details some of the human rights abuses in Tibet under Chinese rule. With Chinese as the dominant language, native Tibetans' access to business, educational and academic careers is limited, and criticism of the Chinese government results in detainment and imprisonment.

Freedom House, "Freedom in the World - Tibet (China) 2007," March 24, 2008. www.freedomhouse.org. Reproduced by permission.

As you read, consider the following questions:

1. According to the authors, how is the Tibet Autonomous Region (TAR) governed? Who is the chairman of the TAR?

2. Do Tibetans have free access to the Internet? What types of information have been censored in Tibet, according to the authors?

3. What types of groups are considered illegal in Tibet? Which groups have been allowed to operate in Tibet?

The Chinese government rules Tibet through administration of the TAR [Tibet Autonomous Region] and 10 Tibetan autonomous prefectures in what were traditional Tibetan areas in nearby Sichuan, Qinghai, Gansu and Yunnan Provinces. Under the Chinese constitution, autonomous regions have the right to formulate their own regulations and implement national laws and regulations in accordance with local conditions. In practice, the TAR mirrors the rest of China and is governed through the local legislature or people's congress system, with representatives sent annually to attend the National People's Congress in Beijing. Unlike China's provinces, which are run by a governor, autonomous regional governments have the post of chairman, usually held by a member of the largest ethnic group. Jampa Phuntsog, an ethnic Tibetan, has served as chairman of the TAR government since 2003, but few of the other senior positions are held by Tibetans. No Tibetan has ever held the top post of TAR Communist Party secretary. Zhang Qingli, a Han Chinese, was appointed to the post in May 2006. The authorities in the TAR continue to strictly limit basic freedoms guaranteed under the Chinese constitution.

Corruption remains a problem in Tibet. In October 2006, Tibet University students demonstrated against official corruption and discrimination in the allocation of civil service jobs to predominantly Han Chinese, a major cause of discontent among ethnic Tibetan graduates. International concerns have also been raised about criminal organizations using the new Qinghai-Tibet railway to smuggle endangered plant and animal species. . . .

Internet Censorship

China controls the flow of information in Tibet, tightly restricting all media and regulating Internet use. Tibetan-language radio programming by Voice of America, Radio Free Asia (RFA), and the Norway-based Voice of Tibet are jammed along with their Chinese-language counterparts. Increased availability of the Internet in urban areas has provided some Tibetans with more access to information, although people must show identity cards before using the Internet in public facilities.

An update to the 2000 restrictions on Internet content was introduced in late September 2005 as a way of preventing the distribution of uncensored information through Web sites or e-mail, including all news related to "politics, economics, military affairs, foreign affairs and social and public affairs." This ban includes any information relating to Tibetan independence, the government-in-exile, and human rights abuses. In April 2005, the Tibet Culture Web site was closed down, and in October 2006, a series of online blogs written by Tibetan poet and intellectual Oeser was also closed by the Chinese authorities. A media clampdown under way throughout China is being enforced all the more strictly in ethnic minority areas, including Tibet.

Religion Is Suppressed

According to the U.S. State Department's 2005 human rights report, issued in March 2006, the government's record on respect for religious freedom "remained poor." While some religious practices are tolerated, officials "forcibly suppressed activities they viewed as vehicles for political dissent or advocacy of Tibetan independence." Possession of pictures of the Dalai

Lama can still lead to imprisonment. Communist Party members and senior officials in Tibet must adhere to atheism and cannot practice a religion. The Religious Affairs Bureaus (RABs) continue to control who can and cannot study religion in the TAR. Officials allow only boys over the age of 18 to become monks, and they are required to sign a declaration rejecting Tibetan independence, expressing loyalty to the Chinese government, and denouncing the Dalai Lama. Since 1996, Beijing has strengthened control over monasteries under a propaganda campaign intended to undermine the Dalai Lama's influence as a spiritual and political leader. The government announced the end of this "patriotic education campaign" in 2000, but government-run "work teams" continue to visit monasteries to conduct mandatory sessions. In 2005, 40 out of 50 nuns practicing at the Gyarak Nunnery were expelled for refusing to participate in such sessions. Since Zhang Qingli was appointed Communist Party secretary in Tibet in May 2006, he has called for an intensification of the "patriotic education" campaign for monks and nuns.

The government manages the daily operations of monasteries through Democratic Management Committees (DMCs) and the RABs. The government approves all committee members so that only "patriotic and devoted" monks and nuns may lead DMCs. Since 1995, laypeople have also been appointed to these committees. According to the U.S. State Department's 2005 human rights report, released in March 2006, Beijing claims that Buddhist monasteries are associated with pro-independence activism in Tibetan areas. As a result, spiritual leaders have encountered difficulty reestablishing historical monasteries, facing a lack of funds, restrictions on monastic education, and denial of government permission to operate religious institutions.

Other Restrictions

In universities, professors cannot lecture on certain topics, and many must attend political indoctrination sessions. The government restricts course materials, prohibiting information deemed "politically sensitive," in order to prevent campus-based political and religious activity. According to the U.S. State Department, students at Tibet University are barred from religious practice.

Independent trade unions, civic groups, and human rights groups are illegal. Some international nongovernmental organizations (NGOs) focusing on development and health care operate in Tibet, under highly restrictive agreements signed with Chinese government agencies. However, cumbersome registration requirements and the clampdown on NGOs following the "color revolutions" in some former Soviet republics in 2003–05 make it increasingly difficult for these organizations to operate.

While some progress has been made in establishing the rule of law in other parts of China, the judicial system in Tibet remains abysmal, with most judges lacking any legal education. There is a lack of access to legal representation, and trials are closed if the issue of "state security" is invoked. In January 2005, Tenzin Delek Rinpoche, a senior lama sentenced to death in December 2002, had his sentence, which had been temporarily suspended, formally commuted to life in prison under pressure from the international community. In a trial that Human Rights Watch said "lacked any pretense of due process," he was found guilty in 2002 of causing explosions and inciting separatism. His alleged co-conspirator, Lobsang Dondrup, was executed in January 2003.

Crackdown on Asylum Seekers

Following the September 2006 videotaping of Chinese soldiers shooting Tibetan civilians, there has been a crackdown on people trying to flee across the border to Nepal. In October 2006, some 53 Tibetans were detained for allegedly acting as guides for asylum seekers.

Although the Chinese government allowed the UN Human Rights Commission's Special Rapporteur on torture,

Manfred Nowak, to visit Tibet in December 2005, political dissidents continue to face particularly severe human rights abuses. Security forces routinely engage in arbitrary arrest, detention, torture, and execution without due process, punishing even nonviolent protests against Chinese rule. Former detainees who manage to escape overseas after release, such as Jigme Gyatso, recount stories of torture and forced confessions.

Owing to strictly controlled access to the TAR, it is difficult to determine the exact number of political prisoners. According to the 2006 annual report of the U.S. Congressional-Executive Commission on China, there were a total of 103 known political detainees, down from 145 in 2004. However, 24 political detentions took place in 2005, an increase from 15 in 2004. In January 2006, two monks and three nuns were sentenced to up to three years' imprisonment for distributing posters critical of the Chinese government. Separately, Phuntsog Nyidron [a Tibetan Buddhist nun] was permitted to travel to the United States for medical treatment in March 2006, having served 14 years in prison for participating in a peaceful political protest.

> *"The People's Congress of Tibet Autonomous Region and its Standing Committee have stipulated over 230 local laws and regulations, which as a result, fully guaranteed the legitimate rights and interests of people of all ethnic backgrounds in the region."*

Tibet's Civil and Political Rights Are Protected by the Chinese Central Government

Chamba Phuntsok

Chamba Phuntsok is a Tibetan native and the Chinese-appointed governor of the Tibet Autonomous Region (TAR) of the People's Republic of China (PRC). In the following viewpoint, taken from a speech given to the Institute of Foreign Affairs in Nepal, Phuntsok asserts that, with the support of the Chinese Central Government, the Tibet Autonomous Region has been "emancipated," with a transformation in social systems that have turned "former serfs and slaves into masters of the country and society."

Chamba Phuntsok, "Speech by H.E. Chamba Phuntsok, Governor of the People's Government of Tibet Autonomous Region of the People's Republic of China," Institute of Foreign Affairs, Nepal, December 12, 2005. Reproduced by permission.

As you read, consider the following questions:

1. According to Phuntsok, the Tibet Autonomous Region has a population [in 2005] of over 2.7 million. What percentage of these are Tibetan ethnics?

2. According to the author, the Constitution of the People's Republic of China bestowed voting rights to Tibetans. Which officials can they vote for and at what levels of government?

3. According to the author, all local laws, regulations, resolutions, and documents are published in the Tibetan language. Is the Tibetan language also taught in the schools?

Tibet Autonomous Region of China is my hometown. For years, I have been working and living there. Located in Southwest China, Tibet Autonomous Region boasts the highest river in the world, that is the Yaluzanbujiang River, the cradle of the Tibetan ethnic group, the Yaluzanbu Great Valley is the highest valley and the magnificent Mount Everest is the highest peak in the world. The well-known Potala Palace, Jokhang Temple, Norblanka have been listed as world cultural heritages by UNESCO (United Nations Educational, Scientific and Cultural Organization). The altitude of my hometown averages over 4,000 meters, which used to be described as the roof of the world or the third pole on earth. Tibet Autonomous Region covers an area of more than 1.2 million square kilometers, with a population of over 2.7 million. Among them, over 92 percent are Tibetan ethnics.

In the last forty years since its founding, under the generous and un-selfish support from the Central Government and people nationwide, and through the hard work of people of all ethnic backgrounds in the region, the productive forces of Tibet Autonomous Region have been greatly emancipated and seen impressive progress, with world-noted accomplishment in its economic and social development, dramatic changes in

Tibetans Manage State and Local Affairs

Citizens of the Tibet Autonomous Region who have reached the age of 18 have the right to vote and to stand for election, regardless of their ethnic status, race, sex, occupation, family background, religious belief, education, property status, or length of residence. They can directly vote for deputies to the people's congresses of counties, districts, townships and towns. These deputies can in turn elect deputies to the national, autonomous regional and municipal people's congresses. The people exercise the power of managing the state and local affairs through the people's congresses at all levels. The political enthusiasm of the Tibetan people is high because they have obtained the right to be masters of their own affairs. They have actively exercised their rights.

Government White Papers,
"Tibet—Its Ownership And Human Rights Situation, vi.
The People Enjoy Political Rights," May 20, 2008. www.china.org.

its urban and rural areas, during its modernization drive. The total GDP [Gross Domestic Product] of the region reached over 24 billion yuan, a 20-fold increase of that in 1965, with a per capital GDP of more than 8000 yuan.

In the last forty years, the Central Government has earmarked a huge amount of investment to improve the infrastructure of the region. The poor traffic in the region, where horses and mules used to serve as the daily transport tools, has turned into a modern communication and transport network linked by highways, civil aviation and tunnels. The mileage of highways reached 43,700 kilometers. . . .

Social Security Improved

With constant economic and social progress, the incomes of people in both urban and rural areas have upgraded by a big margin. The living standards of ordinary people have greatly improved accordingly. [In 2005] the per capita net income of farmers and herdsmen reached over 2000 yuan. The per capita living space of farmers and herdsmen reached 21.3 square meters and for urban residents, 20.11 square meters. With the support and assistance of the government, a gradually improved social security mechanism has been put into place, as a result, the pensions of the retired in state-owned enterprises and minimum wages of urban residents have been upgraded. The mechanism of unemployment insurance and insurance for on-duty injuries as well as criteria for minimum wages has been set up. The special medical care and aid system to the people under extreme poverty has been put into place. . . .

The Rights of Autonomy

China is a large family with fifty-six ethnic groups in the country. It is one of the important political systems of China to apply the system of regional national autonomy in areas populated by minority nationalities, by which minority ethnic groups in China fully enjoy the rights of running the state and local affairs. As stipulated in the Constitution of the People's Republic of China and Law on Regional National Autonomy of the People's Republic of China, local governments in autonomous regions of China enjoy the same jurisdiction rights as those in other regions. In addition, they also enjoy the rights of autonomy in governing local internal affairs. After its founding in 1965, under the leadership of the Central Government, Tibet Autonomous Region has seen historical transformation in social systems, and has adopted the system of regional national autonomy, which turned the former serfs and slaves into masters of the country and society. In the last four decades, people of all ethnic groups in Tibet Autonomous Region are enthusiastic in exercising their voting rights bestowed by the Constitution and laws, actively participating in the voting of deputies to the people's congresses at both local and national levels, and running local and state affairs through their elected deputies. The People's Congress of Tibet Autonomous Region and its Standing Committee have stipulated over 230 local laws and regulations, which as a result, fully guaranteed the legitimate rights and interests of people of all ethnic backgrounds in the region. In the last forty years, there have been altogether seven chairmen for the People's Government of Tibet Autonomous Region. With no exception, all the seven are citizens of Tibetan ethnics. The practice in the last four decades fully demonstrates that the regional national autonomy system of China is in conformity with the reality of China including Tibet Autonomous Region, and is overwhelmingly welcomed and supported by people of all ethnic groups in the region. I myself have turned from a son of a peasant family into the incumbent chairman of the region. My own story is a vivid testimony and demonstration of the fact that people of all ethnic backgrounds have become masters of the region and country.

Language and Culture Respected

The Central Government attaches great importance to the heritage and development of traditional culture, and has adopted the policy of freedom in religious belief and all schools of religion are equal. The religious freedom and traditional folk customs of the Tibetan ethnic group are fully respected and well protected. . . .

All official papers including the publication of local laws, regulations, resolutions and documents, are written in Tibetan language. All billboards of government's departments and in public places must have Tibetan language. Local courts and procurators are required to handle lawsuits involving Tibetan ethnic clients in Tibetan language, and all legal documents are required to be written in Tibetan language. Tibetan language studies are required by all schools in the region as a major. . . .

"Big Family of the Motherland"

Under the leadership of the Central Government and in a big family of motherland, people of all ethnic groups in the region fully enjoy autonomy politically, economically and socially, and fully enjoy free choices in developing traditional culture and freedom in religious belief. . . .

Tibet Autonomous Region today enjoys political stability, rapid economic development, impressive social progress harmonious national unity and peaceful border where people are content with their living and daily life. It is the best historical period of the region in terms of its development and stability after the middle period of last century. In the past forty years since the founding of Tibet Autonomous Region, people of all ethnic backgrounds in the region have been feeling deeply the warmth of a big family of motherland, become more determined to turn their hometown into a more beautiful one, safeguard national unity, and seek common prosperity among all ethnic groups. We are fully confident that with the special care of Central Government and generous support of people nationwide, with the solid foundation paved in its forty-year modernization drive, along with the hard-working of 2.7 million people of all ethnic backgrounds in the region, the future of Tibet Autonomous Region will become more promising and prosperous.

Periodical Bibliography

The following articles have been selected to supplement the diverse views presented in this chapter.

Asian Labour News	"High Wages in Tibet Benefit the Privileged," February 21, 2005. www.hartford-hwp.com.
Dinah Gardner	"Tibet Seen Through Chinese Eyes," May 29, 2008. www.aljajeera.net.
Lindsey Hilsum	"Tibet: Death by Consumerism," *New Statesman*, August 30, 2007. www.newstatesman.com/asia.
S. D'Montford	"Unveiling Bloody Buddhism," *Nexus Magazine*, vol. 12, no. 4, June–July 2005.
Xeni Jardin	"Exiled Tibetans in Dharamsala Protest Google Censorship in China," *Boing Boing*, February 14, 2006. www.boingboing.net.
Sam Price	"One World, One Dream: I Was Detained for Tibet," *Orato You Are The News*, February 25, 2008. www.orato.com.
Reporters Without Borders	"Dalai Lama's 70th Birthday—Passing Years Bring No Let-Up in Harsh Curbs on Press Freedom," July 5, 2005. www.rsf.org.
Eric Sommer	"Not an Issue of Human Rights," *China Daily*, April 2, 2008.
Lee Hudson Teslik	"Trouble in Tibet," *Council on Foreign Relations*, March 19, 2008. www.cfr.org.
John Walsh	"The Chinese Domination of Tibet: Economic Colonization Trumps Political," August 13, 2007. http://china.suite101.com.
Xinhua News Agency	"China Improves Tibetan Life & Livelihood," *China Through a Lens*, May 8, 2004. www.china.org.cn.

CHAPTER 4

What Are the Major Threats to Survival of Tibet's Natural Environment?

Chapter Preface

Every year since 1642, Tibet's reigning Dalai Lama has issued a "Decree for the Protection of Animals and the Environment." This tradition demonstrates the deep respect for all living beings that is a core value of Tibetan Buddhism.

Since Chinese rule in Tibet began, "Tibet's traditional environment protection system has given way to an 'ecocide' of appalling proportions. The effects of this are especially notable in the grassland areas, the cropland areas, the forests, the water resource and the wildlife," according to a report issued by Tibet's government in exile.

Zhang Yongze, an environmental official with the Chinese government, contends that China is acting to protect Tibet's ecological system. "China is planning to invest more than 10 billion yuan to protect the ecological system of the Tibet Plateau during the 2006–2030 period. Fourteen conservation projects will be launched under the unprecedented program, covering natural grassland and wildlife protection, the establishment of nature reserves, the control of desertification and soil erosion, and geological disasters prevention."

The Tibetan government in exile contends that "Tibet's complex environmental problems cannot be addressed by cosmetic changes like designating swathes of land as nature reserves or making laws for the people when the real perpetrator of environmental damage is the Government itself. There should be political will on the part of the Chinese leadership to restore rights . . . to the Tibetan people and allow them to follow their traditional conservationist practices."

"Tibet's future is shaped by the fundamental conflict between the worldview of Tibetan Buddhism and China's drive to modernize. . . . If China's recent history of environmental stewardship is any guide," argues Fred Schwab, a geology professor at Washington and Lee University, "the future of Tibet is as hazy as Beijing's sky."

On May 12, 2008, an earthquake hit central China. Close to seventy thousand persons were reported killed and many thousands were unaccounted for, while millions were left homeless. The quake was especially devastating to Sichuan province, a region that many Tibetans consider part of their historic territory. Sichuan province is home to many ethnic Tibetan people and is a gateway region to Mount Everest, known to Tibetans as Mount Qomolangma, the highest peak in the world. The Qinghai-Tibet railway, called an "engineering marvel," is built on permafrost on the Tibetan plateau. In its first year of operation, the new rail line transported 1.5 million passengers to the Himalayan region.

Earthquakes and railways and the environmental consequences of Chinese modernization are not the only factors that threaten Tibet's fragile ecosystem, according to Song Shanynn, director of the Tibet Regional Meteorological Bureau. "The warming climate has caused more meteorological disasters than ever in Tibet. Problems like receding snow lines, shrinking glaciers, drying grasslands and desert expansion are increasingly threatening the natural ecosystem in the region," explains Shanynn. The effects of global climate change are dramatically apparent on the Tibetan plateau.

The combination of many factors has placed extreme stress on Tibet's natural environment. Finding agreement on which of the rapid changes occurring in Tibet will cause the gravest threat, and what is the best means to address the environmental consequences of such change, is an ongoing debate. However, there is agreement that urgent measures must be put in place to preserve Tibet's fragile ecosystem and to forestall any further environmental harm.

> "Projects such as the Qinghai-Tibet rail-
> road are likely to bring with them en-
> vironmental problems that will dwarf
> those already faced in Tibet.... While
> the environmental impact of the rail-
> road construction is being mitigated,
> the environmental and social impacts
> that the railroad will bring are not."

The China-Tibet Railway Threatens Tibet's Fragile Ecosystem

Peter Haertling

Peter Haertling is a graduate of the University of Colorado School of Law. He taught English and American culture classes at Xi'an Jiaotong University in the People's Republic of China. In the following viewpoint, Haertling argues that protecting Tibet's environment is interconnected with protecting the politi-cal and civil human rights of the Tibetan people. Haertling con-tends that Tibetans must have a meaningful role in government to raise a serious challenge to China's environmental degrada-

Peter Haertling, "Trains Above the Clouds: The Primacy of Political and Civil Human Rights in Tibet and the People's Republic of China," *Colorado Journal of International Environmental Law & Policy*, vol. 18, Spring 2007, p. 459–476. Copyright © 2007 Colorado Journal of International Environmental Law and Policy. Reproduced by per-mission.

tion in Tibet. In his view, the China-Tibet railway project will only hasten the destruction of the Tibetan environment.

As you read, consider the following questions:

1. Haertling asserts that Tibetan religion and value systems had been instrumental in preserving Tibet's environment prior to Chinese control. According to the author, what are some ways this was accomplished?

2. How much money did China allocate for environmental protection during construction of the Qinghai-Tibet railroad? In the author's opinion, what might China's motivation have been in providing such extensive environmental protection?

3. What kinds of environmental and economic changes, according to the author, may occur as a result of the new railway construction? Will the Tibetan people benefit?

On notable occasions, China has been forced to yield to human rights advocates, environmentalists, and foreign governments when creating domestic policy. One prominent example is China's decision in the 1980s to bring its nuclear program up to international standards of safety and environmental protection. A more recent example is the manner in which the Qinghai-Tibet railroad is being constructed, with a virtually unlimited amount of funds to protect Tibet's fragile environment. . . .

Tibet has clearly undergone a drastic change since the Chinese asserted control in 1949. The years since 1949 have seen an ecological disaster unparalleled in the history of Tibet. Tibet had been, prior to Chinese control, a society based on the subsistence farming of barley. Traditional Tibetan religion and value systems had been instrumental in preserving Tibet's environment. Tibetan Buddhism discouraged over-consumption and over-exploitation of natural resources. The various Dalai Lamas (or depending on who one asks, the various incarnations of the Dalai Lama) have issued a Decree for the Protection of Animals and the Environment once a year since 1642. Environmental protection is still clearly the goal of the current Dalai Lama who has proposed that, given independence, "it would be the Government of Tibet's goal to transform Tibet into our planet's largest natural preserve."

Chinese Rule Leads to Environmental Degradation

When the Chinese nuclear weapons program began in earnest in the early 1960s, Tibet was the natural choice of sites for developing the technology, due primarily to its seclusion. Because of the haste with which China sought to develop nuclear weapons, waste disposal was far from a top priority, and waste was placed in shallow unlined landfills.... Moreover, for economic purposes, in 1984 China agreed to import radioactive waste from Europe, although it is unclear whether or not the plans were ever carried out. There are also nine known uranium mines in Northern Tibet, which may pose serious risks to Tibetans. Little is known about the effects of the Chinese nuclear program on the Tibetan environment because the government forbids researchers from studying the areas.

China's shortage of timber has lead to clear-cutting of many Tibetan forests. In parts of Tibet, nearly 70 percent of the forest has been cut. Non-native trees are used in reforestation efforts, destroying the bio-diversity of Tibet's forests. Soil erosion, higher daily temperature ranges, and decreased agricultural production have all been observed in Tibet due to deforestation. Large-scale damming operations have displaced some Tibetans from their homes, and done untold damage to the environment.

Despite all of this damage to Tibet's environment, the worst may be yet to come. Tibet has become a particular focus of Chinese development plans, with 90 percent of its provincial budget coming from the Chinese central government. China's Vice-Premier, Zeng Peiyan, stated that China's "western development" program is expected to change only by the increased speed at which it will be implemented. Furthermore, he pointed to the Qinghai-Tibet railroad as an example of the sort of program that is needed to further develop western China. Projects such as the Qinghai-Tibet railroad are likely to bring with them environmental problems that will dwarf those already faced in Tibet. . . .

A Marvel of Modern Engineering

The Qinghai-Tibet railroad is a marvel of modern engineering. From Qinghai, it will run 685 miles to the capital of Tibet, Lhasa. The turbocharged engines will power the pressurized cars of the train over the so-called "roof of the world" at altitudes many planes are incapable of reaching. The train will often run literally above the clouds. It will service the world's highest train stop, Tangula Shankou, which is 16,640 feet above sea level. The workers constructing the railroad must wear oxygen masks in order to breathe. On board, patrons will enjoy a spa or dine in one of several gourmet restaurants. Tentatively, the first train should pass through the route in 2007. One might think that the Chinese government would be quick to show off this marvel. Yet China is acting downright modest about its achievement, denying press passes to foreign press, and refusing to answer questions about the railroad.

In uncharacteristic style for a Chinese government that regularly puts economic development well before environmental protection, China has allocated $240 million of the $3.1 billion dollars budgeted for the railroad, for environmental protection. China even went so far as to create 20 acres of replacement wetlands, when it was discovered that part of the habitat for black-neck cranes would be destroyed by the railroad construction. Yang Xin, a Chinese environmentalist, has called the project one of the "most caring" he has seen. Appar-

Fast Track to Oblivion

The railway through Tibet is most likely the most expensive ever constructed, costing over US $4.1 billion to lay 1,130 km of track. Half of that track is constructed over permafrost terrain—another world first. And for a number of reasons—environmental, demographical—the line is the holder of a more dubious honour. It is the world's most controversial railway. . . .

The Tibet railway was constructed over the period 2001 to 2005: it cost more over that four-year period than the entire budget spent in Tibet on education and health care since it was invaded by China in 1950. The railway was not built for philanthropic purposes: it was built to exploit the untapped natural resources of Tibet, and to tighten Beijing's control over the troubled region. . . .

Over 550 km of track has been constructed over fragile permafrost terrain. A project of this scale over permafrost has not been attempted elsewhere: it is unknown what environmental shocks are in store. An immediate dilemma is posed for migrating animals, like the highly endangered Tibetan antelope. Sections of the line are elevated, with fencing in place to stop yaks wandering onto the tracks: this forms a kind of mini Great Wall across northern Tibet. To get past the barrier, engineers have thoughtfully built culverts for animals to pass under the tracks. But while yaks can certainly be coaxed through such culverts by herders, wild animals might not be so easily persuaded.

Michael Buckley, "A Railway Runs Through It,"
Perceptive Travel, *July–August 2006. www.perceptivetravel.com.*

ently, the Chinese government even gave consideration to environmental protection plans recommended by NGOs [nongovernmental organizations]. According to Yang, "[NGOs] proposed detailed measures on protecting migrating Tibetan antelopes in the morning, and to our surprise we got the government's answer back that very afternoon, less than three hours later."

The apparent explanation for both China's humbleness regarding the railroad, as well as the facility's environmentally sensitive construction, is the very reason the railroad is being constructed. While the environmental impact of the railroad construction is being mitigated, the environmental and social impacts that the railroad will bring are not. The railroad is a continuation of China's half-century long population transfer policy, seeking to dilute the native Tibetan population with Han Chinese people, thereby destroying any further rumblings from the Tibetan independence movement. The railroad would also greatly facilitate movement of the Chinese army into Tibet, should the independence movement flair up again. Providing for extensive environmental protections may be a strategic ploy to ensure human rights observers are not handed further ammunition against the Chinese policy. Indeed, if one looks at the project through a simple environmental lens, one might see the railroad as a great example of how governments should conduct large-scale development projects in an environmentally sensitive manner. But, if one stops to consider the way in which the Tibetan people's political and civil human rights have been systematically repressed, the railroad can be seen as a tool for the further exploitation and destruction of the Tibetan environment. . . .

The End of Tibet

The situation in Tibet illustrates the primacy of political and civil human rights in realizing cultural, economic, and environmental rights. Tibetans have no true voice in their government, and are therefore unable to protest Chinese policies or air their concerns. Summarizing the Tibetans' views on the

Qinghai-Tibet railroad, Dr. Robert Barnett, a professor of Modern Tibetan Studies at Columbia said, "in public, Tibetans will not voice any criticism. But in private, they will tell you that this is the end of Tibet." Denied a meaningful voice in government, any semblance of due process, and subject to lengthy prison sentences for advocating independence or supporting the Dalai Lama, Tibetans are forced to accept whatever environmental policy Beijing proscribes. That policy, far from the Dalai Lama's policy of turning Tibet into the "world's largest natural preserve," has tragic results for both the people and the environment of Tibet.

The construction of the railroad is certain to bring about a drastic increase in the amount of mining, along with associated and inevitable environmental degradation. Large-scale mining in Tibet began shortly after the 1949 Chinese assertion of power. In the vicinity of the railroad route, thirteen new copper belts, with more than 1 million tons of copper have been found. In addition, two cobalt deposits with around 20,000 tons of cobalt have been discovered. The mining done inside of Tibet is carried out almost exclusively by Han Chinese, and most of the finished product is exported out of Tibet.

China asserts that Tibetans are benefiting greatly from the increased economic activity that its policies have brought. The railroad, according to the Chinese government, will only intensify this benefit. While it is undoubtedly true that some Tibetans have obtained higher living standards due to Chinese economic development of the region, it seems fair to question how benign China's interest in developing Tibet's economy is, and just who is actually benefiting from the development. Once again, the Qinghai-Tibet railroad proves illustrative. The construction of the railroad created 38,000 new jobs, of which Tibetans received only 4,000–5,000. Tibetans working on the railroad were promised the equivalent of $30 U.S. dollars a day, but instead received only between $9 and $12 dollars. No

Tibetan has received a single one of the skilled positions, which pays as much as $2,500 a month. According to some Tibetans, the Chinese government has told them that certain jobs are "not open to Tibetans." There are also reports of young girls turning to prostitution in the wake of the influx of railroad laborers. The Tibetan government-in-exile asserts that construction of hydroelectric dams in Tibet similarly excludes Tibetans from securing jobs. It has also been noted that the electricity generated by the dams goes primarily to benefit Chinese immigrants, while most Tibetans continue to live without electricity. . . .

The Chinese environmental exploitation of Tibet is at odds with the history of Tibet, the Tibetan culture, and the express wishes of their spiritual (and arguably political) leader the Dalai Lama. Far from becoming the "world's largest natural preserve," Tibet appears to be headed toward similar levels of environmental degradation observed in the whole of China. Without the ability to assert their political will against the government of China, neither Tibetans nor the citizens of mainland China are likely to have any success in protecting or improving their respective natural environments. . . .

Given the interconnectedness of environmental rights and political and civil human rights, only by securing a meaningful role in government, and creating meaningful protections against arbitrary governmental action can the international community and the Chinese people protect China's environment, culture, and economy.

> *"The Tibetan Plateau has a unique and fragile ecosystem, so 33 animal underpasses were constructed. . . . In order to protect the environment during the life of the railway's operation, the trains are designed as a closed system to protect the environment it passes through."*

The China-Tibet Railway Does Not Threaten Tibet's Fragile Ecosystem

James C. Cobb, Lanmin Wang, Edward W. Woolery, Zhenming Wang, Zhijan Wu

James Cobb is the director of the Kentucky Geological Survey in Lexington and Lanmin Wang is the director of the Lanzhou Institute of Seismology in China. Edward Woolery and Zhenming Wang are seismologists and Zhijan Wu works with both the Kentucky Geological Survey and the Lanzhou Institute of Seismology in China. In the following viewpoint, the authors detail the precautions taken to protect the fragile Tibetan plateau during construction of the Qinghai-Tibet Railway. They contend that care was taken to protect the permafrost and to mitigate seismic hazards.

James C. Cobb, et al., "Rolling Across the Roof of the World," *GeoTimes*, February, 2007. Reproduced by permission.

As you read, consider the following questions:

1. According to the authors, what is the length of the China-Tibet Railway? How many mountain chains does it traverse?

2. According to the viewpoint, what was the most pervasive challenge for both construction and maintenance of the railway? If the challenge is not met, what might occur?

3. During the 2001 magnitude 8.1 earthquake in Tibet, how long was the surface rupture near the Kunlun Pass?

China made history on July 1, 2006, when the Qinghai-Tibet Railway opened for passenger service. The railway is the highest-elevation passenger train in the world and the first to connect central China with Tibet, providing a controversial but arguably economically significant link between Tibet and the rest of China. Stretching about 1,142 kilometers, the railway runs from Golmud in China's Qinghai province to Lhasa, Tibet's capital. Most of its length is above 4,000 meters in elevation, and 50 kilometers is above 5,000 meters.

The railway traverses the spectacular topography of the Tibetan Plateau, cutting across four mountain chains—Kunlun, Fenghuo, Tanggula and Nianqintanggula—where elevations of the trackbed are all above 4,600 meters. It also crosses five major rivers—the Yellow, Yangtse, Mekong (Lancang), Nujiang and Lhasa-Brahmaputra—and passes through the Three Rivers National Natural Protection Region, an area known for its biological diversity, geological and landscape variety, and scenic beauty in southwestern China.

At 4,650 meters elevation on the Tibetan Plateau, with atmospheric pressure and oxygen 45 percent lower than at sea level, an annual average air temperature of 5 degrees below zero Celsius, and extremes including low temperatures of negative 47.8 degrees Celsius and wind speeds above 30 meters per second, this is a harsh climate. Add in solar and ultraviolet radiation 1.5 to 2.5 times what it is at sea level, and not only is preconstruction research and fieldwork a challenge, but so is the construction itself.

Major Obstacles

In addition, construction of the railway, which began in 2001, had to contend with major geotechnical challenges such as environmental protection, permafrost and geologic hazards, such as steep and unstable slopes, variable hydrologic conditions and seismic activity. But the completion of the railroad across the so-called roof of the world is likely to remain one of the most outstanding geotechnical achievements of the 21st century. And we, a group of researchers from the University of Kentucky (UK) and the Lanzhou Institute of Seismology (LIS), were fortunate to have been a part of this exciting project, at least in small part. Interestingly, none of us had worked at such a high elevation before—4,700 meters—and adjusting to the conditions wasn't easy. In the course of a few hours, it was sunny and warm, then rained, sleeted, snowed, and was sunny again. Such are the weather and the working conditions in this remarkable area.

The Permafrost Problem

The railway crosses the largest area of low-latitude permafrost in the world. (Surprising to some people is that Lhasa, Tibet, lies at 30 degrees north latitude—the same as Houston, Texas.) Stabilizing permafrost was the most pervasive challenge for both construction and maintenance of the railway. Nearly 550 kilometers of the railway are built over permafrost. Protecting the permafrost is key to preventing embankment and roadbed failure from frost heaving and thaw collapse. If the permafrost absorbs thermal energy that is not dissipated, then the permafrost will melt and the roadbed will be damaged. . . .

Protecting the permafrost along the railway was accomplished using both traditional and less-used approaches. Much

Environmental Protection Essential Concern in Rail Design

When completed, the stations along the Qinghai-Tibet Railway will use environment-friendly energy sources such as electricity, solar energy and wind energy for heating. Garbage at the stations will be collected for batch treatment. Domestic sewage, after being treated to meet the State's discharge standard, will be used, whenever possible, to water green spaces. The passenger cars will be sealed. Garbage on the trains will be collected in plastic bags, which will be handed over to stations along the plateau for batch treatment. To suit the characteristics of the plateau, the central station management mode will be adopted, with seven central stations established along the line. Each of these stations will be totally responsible for the trains' running and maintenance in an area within a radius of 80 km. Wherever possible, remote automatic control and mechanized maintenance will be adopted to reduce the number of both the organizations and their staff on the plateau, thereby giving maximum protection to the natural eco-environment of the Qinghai-Tibet Plateau.

Embassy of the People's Republic of China in the United States,
"White Paper: Ecological Improvement and Environmental
Protection in Tibet," March 10, 2003. www.china-embassy.org.

of the embankments and roadbeds are protected with "riprap," which is coarse, angular pieces of rock used to stabilize a surface. The riprap-engineering measures both shield the roadbeds and embankments from solar heating and cool them by convection to maintain a higher thaw depth, which thus protects the permafrost. The larger rock sizes—10 to 15 centimeters and 40 to 50 centimeters—and the large spaces between rocks are the key to increasing cooling energy and heat exchange under the riprap. The penetration of the cold energy is two to four times greater with the riprap than through normal graded roadbeds.

Other approaches are also used, including bridges, ventilated-pipe roadbed, awning-covered roadbed, and protecting the roadbed with heat pipes. Heat pipes are used on the Qinghai-Tibet Railway for the same reason they are used on the Trans-Alaska Pipeline: to stabilize permafrost by removing heat from the permafrost and dissipating it into the ambient cold air. The advantage of heat pipes is their efficiency in transferring heat. They employ evaporative cooling to transfer thermal energy from one point to another by the evaporation and condensation of a coolant. Heat pipes rely on a temperature difference between the ends of the pipe and cannot lower temperatures at either end beyond the ambient temperature. A total of 30 kilometers of the railway have heat-pipe-protected roadbed, which is particularly effective given the frigid temperatures.

In a slightly different approach, the ventilated-pipe-protected roadbed has an open pipe installed beneath the roadbed through the embankment that cools the ground, as denser cold air flows into the pipes and displaces less dense, warmer air. Any accumulation of heat will be carried away through the pipe, thus maintaining the frozen permafrost.

Finally, nothing is perhaps more effective at keeping surface temperatures cool than shade. Because of the strength of solar radiation in this area, sunshades or awnings were constructed to shade the roadbeds and embankments from solar heating. The awnings also prevent rain and snow from directly impacting the roadbed.

Seismic Work

Seismic activity is another important factor in the design of the Qinghai-Tibet Railway, as earthquakes can be both frequent and strong in the Tibetan Plateau. This is where our team in particular came in, as we have been working together to assess seismic hazards and recommend mitigation measures.

On November 14, 2001, a magnitude-8.1 earthquake created a surface rupture 430 kilometers long near the Kunlun Pass. In July 2006, a joint LIS-UK research team conducted field investigations using the shear-wave seismic method where the railway crosses the Kunlun Fault, hoping to characterize the fault—especially its width—close to the train track.

The profile closest to the track showed the fault segment to have spread about 50 meters wide under extensional forces. About 200 meters to the west, the other profile showed the fault to have squeezed together under compression, and is less than 20 meters wide. The shear-wave method worked well in this area imaging a section of permafrost and possible lacustrine and colluvial sediments about 30 meters thick. The railway engineers can use this data to design mitigation measures to safeguard the track from future displacements on the fault triggered by seismic events.

Environmental Sensitivity

The Tibetan Plateau has a unique and fragile ecosystem, so 33 animal underpasses were constructed. Additionally, to minimize environmental disturbance during construction, staging areas were planned to minimize surface disturbance and avoid sensitive areas, and were revegetated at the completion of the construction. In order to protect the environment during the life of the railway's operation, the trains are designed as a closed system to protect the environment it passes through. The train cars are closed, so no waste, litter or discharges are allowed or even possible from the cars. All refuse is contained on board the train for disposal at the stations. . . .

The new rail connection to Tibet is a remarkable geotechnical achievement, encompassing extensive geologic and engineering efforts. The Qinghai-Tibet Railway brings greater access to the Tibetan Plateau—which is good news to geoscientists wanting to see this fantastic and still remote part of the world.

> *"The biggest injury to the land has been the conversion of marginal pastures into land for agriculture by Chinese settlers. Often resulting in desertification of the land—the land is no longer fit for grazing or agriculture."*

Chinese Rule Is the Greatest Threat to Tibet's Natural Resources

Patrick T. Hughes

Patrick T. Hughes was educated at American University in Washington, D.C., and Peking University in Beijing, China. He speaks, reads, and writes in Mandarin Chinese. In China, he was a foreign correspondent for The Review *in Plymouth, Wisconsin. In the following viewpoint, Hughes argues that environmental concerns play a large part in the China-Tibet conflict. Hughes contends that it is the Chinese occupation of Tibet that accounts for the downward trend in management and preservation of Tibet's natural resources.*

Patrick T. Hughes, "Environmental Degradation in the Tibetan Autonomous Region," The Inventory of Conflict & Environment (ICE), May, 2006. Reproduced by permission of the author.

As you read, consider the following questions:

1. According to Hughes, how many climate regions are there in Tibet? What is the average elevation of the Tibetan Plateau?

2. How much of Tibet is covered in grasslands, according to the author? How many animals depend on the grassland for sustenance?

3. In the author's view, why is China turning to Tibet in pursuit of minerals? What are some of the environmental harms of mining activity?

There are a number issues surrounding the environment of Tibet. The priority issue of Tibetans is regaining their status as a sovereign nation. This is by far the most volatile topic concerning Tibet, one that has deep roots that extend through both the political and historical landscapes. Although the cause of the conflict cannot be directly attributed to the environment, it is the natural riches of the Tibetan region that make it an attractive portion of land for the Chinese to posses. Many argue that Tibet is an important region to China for two reasons: The first being the ability to access Tibet's vast amount of natural resources. The second is to have a buffer of land separating China from possible western threats, possibly India. Hence, the conflict is indirectly attributed to the environment, however, the environment is a large segment of the conflict.

Varied Climates

Tibet is generally cool and dry, having frigid winter and cool summers. However, it is a complicated landscape that consists of towering mountain peaks that descend down to high altitude plateaus. This makes for a wide variety of climates. Therefore, Tibet is divided into five climate regions: Northern, Southeastern, Central, Yangbajing Thermal area, and the border of South Tibet. Each region has varied climates, in which some at higher altitudes are much colder. Also, some areas receive significantly more precipitation than others. Due to the high altitude, the effects of the sun are very intense.

Situated on the roof of the world, the Tibetan Plateau is the highest and largest plateau in the world. It is a vast expanse of land that rests at an average elevation of 13,000' and stretches for almost 2.5 million sq. kilometers. To the south it is guarded by the Himalayan Mountain chain and to the north the Altyn Tagh and Gangkar Chogley Namgyal Mountains. Its western border merges with the Karakoram Mountains and to the east the Minyak Gangkar and Khawakarpo mountain ranges. The plateau is home to an expansive contrast of landscapes consisting of astral vistas in some parts of Southern Tibet to flourishing tropical forests in Eastern Tibet. It is estimated that 70 percent of Tibet encompassed by rangeland and pasture and 1/10 of its surface area is forest and cropland.

Grasslands

A December of 2005 article on the China Through a Lens Web site, a report released by the China Geological Survey Bureau titled the "Milestone Geological Survey," released less than pleasant news concerning the Tibetan Plateau. It stated that the desert area of the Tibetan Plateau has expanded to 0.5 million square kilometers. Additionally, the report stated that from the 1970s to 2002 the total grassland area shrunk to 24.3 percent and the glacier area decreased 147.36 square kilometers each year.

As much as 70 percent of Tibet is covered in grassland; this natural resource sustains nearly 70 million animals. Furthermore, upwards of a million herdsmen utilize the expansive grasslands to forge out a living, tending to herds of dri, yak, sheep and goats.

The last four decades there has been a significant reduction in these pastures that sustain life and livelihood for both animals and people alike. The biggest injury to the land has been the conversion of marginal pastures into land for agriculture by Chinese settlers. Often resulting in desertification of the land—the land is no longer fit for grazing or agriculture. This problem has been especially prominent in the vast grasslands of Amdo.

The practice of fencing in grasslands has made for significantly less area for Tibetan nomads to engage in their traditional migratory customs. For example, in the Machu district of Amdo, 1/3 of the area of over 10,000 square kilometers has been fenced for the horses, sheep and cattle of the Chinese army. In similar fashion, a majority of the premium pastureland in Ngapa, Golok and "Qinghai" have been reserved for the Chinese.

Forests

Over the past 50 plus years, the Tibetan forests have been severely impacted. In 1949, there was 221,800 square kilometers of forest. By 1985, the forested area was reduced by nearly half, to 134,000 square kilometers. It is reported that $54 billion in timber was removed during that time.

Many of the forests of TAR [Tibet Autonomous Region] grow on steep, isolated slopes in the river valleys of Tibet's low-lying southeastern region. The most commonly found trees in these are the tropical montane and subtropical montane coniferous forest, with spruce, fir, pine, larch, cypress, birch, and oak. The tree line stretches from 3,800 meters in the region's moist south to a towering 4,300 meters in the semi-dry north. Tibet's forests are/were old growth, and not uncommon to find trees 200 years of age. . . .

Deforestation and modern forest management methods not only alter the native landscape but also create a ripple effect of new problems. The removal—often times clear cutting—of over $50 billion in timber since 1959 by the PRC [People's Republic of China] has substantially altered the forests of the Huangho, Yangtse, Mekong, Salween and Brah-

---

Tibet Environment–Conflict Link and Dynamics

The diagram below lists the positive environmental attributes of which the TAR possesses. These are detailed with a (+) sign. The negative effect of the PRC controlling TAR and its relationship to the down turn of the environment is detailed with a (−) sign.

1950
25.2 mil. hectares
of Tibetan forest
+

128 minerals
in Tibet
+

Prior to
PRC control
of Tibet
+

By 2015
15 key minerals
are expected to be
depleted
−

1980
13.57 million
hectares of Tibetan
forests remain
−

1959 China
establishes
control of Tibet
−

70% of Tibet is
rangeland or
pasture land
+

Grasslands
are declining
24.3%
−

TAKEN FROM: "Environment–Conflict Link and Dynamics: Indirect," Environmental Degradation in the Tibetan Autonomous Region, The Inventory of Conflict and Environment (ICE) May, 2006.

---

maputra river valleys. Consequentially, soil erosion, water siltation, habitat loss and climatic effects are the byproduct of deforestation. Hence, there is a potentially volatile future for the water supply of a better portion of Southeast Asia—which makes up nearly a quarter of the world's population.

Water Supply

Tibet is one of Asia's principal watersheds and China has plans to utilize this resource for numerous hydroelectric dams. The electricity generated from Tibet's rivers will be used to power the Chinese cities of Chengdu, Xining, Lanzhou and

Xian. One of the fiercest environmental issues in the recent history of Tibet was a hydroelectric construction project on Yamdrok Tso, a sacred lake between Lhasa and Shigatse. Some were concerned this project could have been one of the largest environmental disasters of the latter portion of the 20th century. The project was completed in the early portion of the 21st century. At one point during the construction of the hydroelectric project, the PRC denied foreigners access to Yamdrok Tso. This was due to the large amount of adverse international attention surrounding the project.

One amazing fact is the 90 percent of TAR's river run-off flows down across its borders out of Tibet, subsequently only 1 percent of this is used within Tibet. As touched on earlier, due to the high levels of deforestation many of Tibet's rivers have developed extremely high sediment rates: The Machu (Huang Ho, or Yellow River), the Tsangpo (Brahmaputra), the Drichu (Yangtze), and the Senge Khabab (Indus) rank among the five most heavily-silted rivers in the world. These rivers irrigate nearly 47 percent of the earth's population, they stretch from the Machu basin in the east to the Senge Khabab to the west.

An argument that is particularly noteworthy is that TAR is one of the world's most optimum locations for solar electric power. Second to only the Sahara Desert with an estimated annual average of 200 kilocalorie/cm, yet the Chinese have set a path to continue to construct dams, which have a far greater impact on the environment.

Minerals

Another indicator of the importance of TAR's natural resources is that between 2000 and 2005 $22.3 billion of minerals were prospected from Tibet. Tibet has a dynamic selection of minerals and ranked first in China for 13 categories of minerals in terms of net output. These minerals include: copper, chromium, boron, sulphur, magnesite, corundum and muscovite.

Furthermore, in 2001 China began to increase mining in Tibet, by aggressively pursuing the gold of TAR. In addition, Australian mining companies and the University of Tasmania are allowed by the PRC to play a large role in the mineral future of Chinese occupied Tibet, as they also look to prosper on the mineral wealth of the region. The Tanjianshan gold deposit, which sits within the northern Tibet's Chokle Namgyal Mountain Range, it is said to hold as much as 41 tons of gold, with a possible value of $335 million.

Nearly half of China's 15 key mineral reserves are expected to be depleted within the next 10 years and major non-ferrous minerals are for all practical spent, China is rapidly moving in on Tibet in pursuit of minerals. Measures to preserve the environment surrounding a mining area are vaguely acknowledged. Areas of particular concern are fragile terrains that often result from mining activity. The creation of fragile terrains can lead to slope destabilization, land degradation, and the opportunity to put human life in harm's way.

Wildlife

Within the Autonomous Region of Tibet, there are 488 species of birds and 142 species of mammals. Moreover, there are 2,307 species of insects, 64 species of fish, 45 species of amphibians, and 55 species of reptiles. Of these, there are 163 rare endangered and valuable species. These consist of 74 species of mammals and 79 species of birds, 4 reptiles, 2 fish, and 2 insects.

Aside from wildlife suffering from hardship due to the loss of habitat resulting from deforestation, polluted waterways, and grasslands slipping into desertification, wildlife are also subject to poachers and sport hunters granted expensive licenses to pursue some of TAR's exotic creatures.

For example, hunting tours are organized and licenses are granted by the PRC for affluent foreign big game hunters. These hunters are granted permission to pursue endangered species such as the Tibetan antelope and the Argali sheep, species that are supposed to be granted the highest level of official protection. The hunts cost up to $35,000 for a Tibetan antelope, $23,000 for an Argali, $13,000 for a white-lipped deer, $7,900 for a blue sheep, and $3,500 for a red deer.

Nuclear Contamination

For several years it was suspected that the PRC was storing weapons and disposing of waste in TAR. In 1993, a Xinhua news report confirmed that there was a 20 sq. meter dump for radioactive pollutants in Haibei Tibetan Autonomous Prefecture, not far from the shores of Lake Kokonor, the largest lake on the Tibetan Plateau.

The nuclear facility known as "Factory 211" is said to be China's premiere nuclear weapons facility. There is much concern that prior to the Xinhua news report, the PRC had been haphazardly disposing nuclear waste materials possibly as early as the late 1960s. The nuclear facility was decommissioned in 1987. . . .

A Level of Strategic Interest

The level of strategic interests for the PRC I would deem to be medium to relatively high. Although Tibet is not yet an industrial area of China, it does supply a vast amount of resources for the mainland of China. TAR also insulates China from the countries of India, Nepal, Burma and Bhutan. Militarily and strategically, China, having the proverbial roof of the world between them and their neighbors, is a convenient buffer zone. With that being said, land amounts to, in many cases, a stockpile of untapped resources. Hence, Tibet is also a reserve of resources for the People's Republic of China to harvest.

For TAR strategically their level of interest is very high, it is land they consider their own. Without control of their land, they are unable to make decisions concerning the maintenance, conservation, and economic use of the resources. For both the PRC and TAR there are numerous reasons why both sides of this would deem the strategic interests of this issue to be relatively high.

As for now, it could be said that China is winning the dispute. It is estimated that 1.2 million have been killed and thousands more jailed since the beginning of the Chinese occupation. The Tibetans do enjoy some autonomy, but ultimately they are under the rule of the People's Republic of China. Essentially, Tibet is one of the last remaining indigenous places on earth. The Chinese occupation of Tibet can be accounted to the downward trend in the management and preservation of Tibet's natural resources.

| "The lives of Tibetans and the many other peoples of the region are dominated by the incredible Himalayas. If glacial retreat continues to accelerate it will be an ecological, economic and social catastrophe." |

Climate Change Is the Greatest Threat to Life on the Tibetan Plateau

Guanli Wang

Guanli Wang is a journalist with the Ministry of Science & Technology of the People's Republic of China. Wang participated in a Greenpeace International expedition to Tibet to gather evidence of the melting of the Rongbuk Glacier, Mount Everest's main glacier. In the following viewpoint, Wang contends that Tibet's shrinking Himalayan glaciers pose a threat not only to Tibetans, but to the nearly one billion people of China, India, Nepal, and Bangladesh.

As you read, consider the following questions:

1. According to the author, what was the plan for the expedition to Mount Everest?

Guanli Wang, "Expedition Documents Melting Himalayan Glaciers," Greenpeace International, June 5, 2007. www.greenpeace.org. Reproduced by permission.

2. In the author's view, why do Tibetan villagers she met not need statistics on climate change to realize something is wrong?

3. In Wang's view, is it too late to avert the climate catastrophe posed by Tibet's melting glaciers? What does she believe is the solution?

I was part of a Greenpeace team, which left Beijing in late April to document glacial retreat on the world's highest peak, Mount Everest (Qomolangma). The plan was to gather visual evidence of the retreat of the Rongbuk Glacier, Everest's main glacier, 5,800 metres above sea level, to build awareness in China of the mounting threat of climate change.

After a four-hour flight, we reached Lhasa, "place of the gods" in Tibetan. Our Tibetan guide Bianba Dunzhu greeted us. Bianba, an instructor with the Tibet Mountaineer Training School, has made it to Everest's summit twice and the world's second highest peak, K2 (Mount Qogir), once.

"Although I am a mountain guide, I dare not conquer Mount Everest too many times. Human beings must respect the holy mountains," Bianba said, recalling the fate of a Nepalese guide who had reached the summit over a dozen times but died at the prime of his life with no obvious cause of death.

Mountainous Rivers

With this reminder to respect the mountains ringing in our ears, we set off from Lhasa, via Shigatse, Tingri and Zaxizong, towards Mount Everest. The expedition also aimed to collect evidence of climate change impacts on the region's rivers. The Himalayas and Qinghai-Tibet plateau are the source of some of the world's major river systems: the Indus, the Ganga-Brahmaputra, Mekong, Yangtze and the Yellow. Almost a billion people live in the watershed areas of these great rivers in China, India, Nepal and Bangladesh.

We saw our first river, the Lhasa River, as we drove from the airport to downtown Lhasa. We were immediately struck by the large deposits of sand on both banks of the river, an indication of the desertification spreading throughout the region. The following day, we crossed the Brahmaputra River. Once famous for its abundant runoff, the flow of the Brahmaputra is now much reduced, with many shallow sections visible.

As we neared Everest, we saw the Rongbuk River, formed by melt water from the Rongbuk Glacier, the area's largest. Forty years ago, the annual runoff of the Rongbuk was around 100 million cubic metres. Now the flow is greatly reduced due to the rapid retreat of the Rongbuk Glacier.

The Qinghai-Tibet Plateau has a staggering 46,298 glaciers. However, recent surveys via remote sensing and fieldwork have recorded a 10 percent reduction in the last three decades, from 48,860 square kilometres (18,865 square miles) in the 1970s to 44,438 square kilometres (17,158 square miles) today. The alarming acceleration of the retreat is being attributed to increased global warming.

At an altitude of 5,200 metres (17,060 feet), the tiny village of Zaxizong stands at the entrance of the Mount Everest Nature Reserve. A small, nearly dry river runs past the village. Renzeng, a 48-year-old farmer tells us that generations of villagers have relied on the river for crop irrigation and their water supply. Renzeng adds, "Now, due to lack of irrigation, the yield of highland barley in our village is less than half what it used to be."

Nearing Everest

Onward and upwards towards Mount Everest, we stop at the Rongbuk Temple, at 5,030 metres (16,503 feet), the highest temple in the world and the best place to view the majestic peak.

Map of the Tibetan Plateau

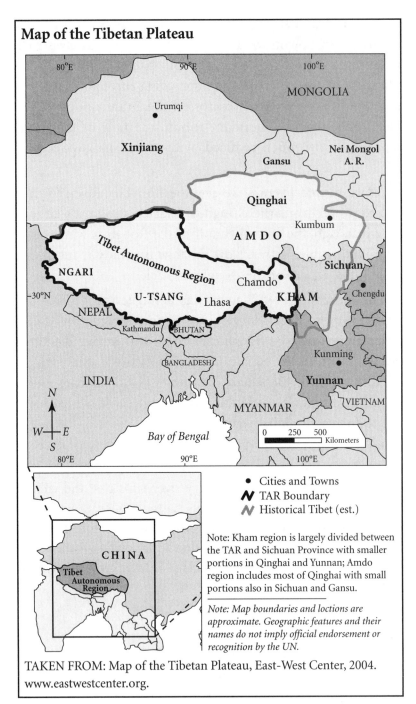

TAKEN FROM: Map of the Tibetan Plateau, East-West Center, 2004.
www.eastwestcenter.org.

The Tibetan name for Everest, Qomolangma, means 'Goddess', and she unveiled herself gracefully, a vision of pure beauty. In Tibetan paintings, Qomolangma is always depicted wearing a white gown and riding a white lion through ice and snow.

The Chief lama of the Rongbuk Temple has been at the temple for 20 years and has witnessed the impacts of climate change first-hand. "I have noticed a reduction in the flow of the Rongbuk River every year and each year is hotter than the last. I am worried about the harsh future our children will suffer," he tells us. Other lamas tell us that before they used to have to force their way through chest high snow, however, now the winter snow only reaches their shins. We leave the temple and head towards the base camp of Mount Everest.

From Everest Base Camp

April is the most popular month for mountain climbing and we see dozens of tents dotted around the camp, temporary homes for mountaineers from across the globe. Heavy snow falls on our first night at the base camp. At 6 a.m. the next morning, we set off through the fresh, boot-high snowfall towards the Rongbuk Glacier, with the aim of completing a whole day of shooting and returning to the base camp before nightfall.

The Rongbuk Glacier flows north and into the Rongbuk Valley north of Mount Everest. The main goal of our expedition is to reach the anchor point left by a 1968 Chinese Academy of Sciences expedition, and take photographs to compare the state of the glacier then and now. Our route takes us from the fork in the road near the base camp, towards the west side of the Rongbuk Glacier across its ridge and north along the west ridge towards Guangming Peak.

Bianba warns us to watch out for falling rocks from the west ridge because of the rapid noontime snow melt. Our map tells us to expect to meet two glaciers on our way. The map shows the two glaciers descending from the 6,927 metres (22,726 feet) Hongxing Peak, which lies to the west of Everest, then running east to join the Rongbuk Glacier.

Instead, we only come across large rocks and debris from a huge landslide where the second glacier was supposed to be. The landslide totally blocks our way and we have to give up, although our destination is only 30 minutes' walk away. As our cameramen work beside a nearby melt-water lake, they heed Bianba's earlier warning as large chunks of ice and snow and a rain of rocks fall close by.

The serac forests of the Rongbuk Glacier amazed Chinese scientists in the 1970s. Seracs are large blocks and columns of ice found near glacial crevasses formed by the glacier moving or melting. At the time one of the scientists wrote, "With a great variety of shapes and forms, the serac forests there made us linger with no intent to leave. Those between 5,300 metres and 6,500 metres are extraordinarily beautiful and fantastic, like an 'ice sculpture park.'"

Today we find a serac forest at 5,600 metres (18,372 feet), but it is sparse, small and worn. The huge 'ice mushrooms' which we expect to see towering above our heads have almost disappeared.

"When I first climbed Mount Everest in 2000, I saw serac forests at 5,400 metres," our guide Bianba tells us. "When I climbed the mountain again in 2006, I only found the serac forests from 5,800 metres." The disappearance of glaciers, large-scale landslides, rock falls and sparse serac forests are all clear examples of climate change.

When our Tibetan porters, who initially thought we were a team of mountaineers, learn of our mission, they excitedly ask our cameramen to record them talking about their respect for nature, conservation of water resources and love of life.

Melting Glaciers

Himalayan glaciers could shrink from the present 500,000 square kilometres (193,051 square miles) to 100,000 square kilometres (38,610 square miles) by the 2030s. The February 2007 release of the Intergovernmental Panel on Climate Change (IPCC) report on the science of climate change concluded, with a 90 percent certainty, that global warming is caused by human behaviour. The report galvanised the European Union to set a target of reducing carbon emissions by at least 20 percent from 1990 levels by 2020, and by 30 percent if other industrialised nations set similar targets.

The Tibetan villagers, farmers, porters and lamas that we met don't need statistics to know that something is very wrong. The close bond that they have with the environment they rely on teaches them to watch the signs—these catastrophic changes have been unfolding before them every day.

The Qinghai-Tibet Plateau covers an area of 2.9 million square kilometres (1.1 million square miles), roughly three times the combined area of the United Kingdom, France and Germany. The Kunlun and Qilian mountains in the north, the Tanglha Mountains in the east and the Himalayas in the south and west border the plateau, with an average altitude of 4,500 metres (14,764 feet).

Only one percent of land on the plateau is arable and crop yields are limited by the dry, cold climate. Although these conditions appear harsh to outsiders, the local Tibetans treasure, revere and celebrate this land.

Tibet

Tibetans have created and maintained their own living philosophy based on obeying nature, cherishing it and feeling awe for it. Using dreamlike imagination and fantastic myths, Tibetans express their deepest love for their homeland. Every Tibetan is born into Buddhism. To them, every living creature has a soul. The body can die but the soul will live forever.

Lhasa's Jokhang Temple, the oldest in Tibet and built by King Songtsan Gampo when he married the Tang Dynasty Princess Wen Cheng more than 1,400 years ago, is always crowded with pilgrims. Buddhism's most famous mantra, "Om Mani Padme Hum,"can be heard everywhere. Tibetans worship the lion, yak, macaque monkey, horse, dog, fish, bird and even plants, but above all, they worship mountains. Surrounded by high mountains, they feel that they are very tiny and trivial.

Tibetan culture and the amazing environment of the region have merged seamlessly. The spirit of Buddhism and local culture is in the blood of local people and it shapes their attitude towards nature. The lives of Tibetans and the many other peoples of the region are dominated by the incredible Himalayas. If glacial retreat continues to accelerate it will be an ecological, economic and social catastrophe.

A Way Forward

It's not too late to avert the climate catastrophe. As well as documenting climate impacts—the costs of doing nothing, Greenpeace is calling for an Energy Revolution, a critical shift in the way we produce and use energy. The solution is to urgently switch investment from climate changing and dangerous energy sources such as coal, oil, gas and nuclear, into sustainable, clean renewable energy sources like wind and solar, combined with a programme of energy efficiency measures.

The alternative? There isn't one. Otherwise, we have to live with the fact that we stood by and did nothing as billions of people suffered and a unique environment was destroyed.

Periodical Bibliography

The following articles have been selected to supplement the diverse views presented in this chapter.

Central Tibetan Administration	"Tibet: A Human Development and Environmental Report," Environment and Development Desk, Department of Information and International Relations.
Richard Gere	"Railroad To Perdition," *The New York Times*, July 15, 2006.
Zia Haq	"Tibetans Say China Forcing Them to Flout Wildlife Laws," *Hindustan Times*, January 31, 2008.
Tseten Norbu	"Railway and China's Development Strategy in Tibet: A Tale of Two Economies," Tibetan Center for Human Rights and Democracy, Interview No. 11, September 12, 2006. www.tchrd.org.
Planet Ark	"As Quake Draws Focus, China Keeps Tibet Under Thumb," June 5, 2008. www.planetark.com.
Wu Qi	"Tibet Boosts Ecological Protection for Purity of 'Roof of the World,'" China Features, May 5, 2008. Embassy of the People's Republic of China in the Arab Republic of Egypt. http://eg.china-embassy.org.
Fred Schwab	"Railway Makes Room for Tibetan Culture: Experts," Chinese Government's Official Web Portal, July 1, 2006.
David Wolman	"Train to the Roof of the World," *Wired*, July 2006. www.wired.com.
Xinhua News Agency	"Global Warming Threatening Tibet's Environment," November 21, 2007. www.chinagate.com.cn.

For Further Discussion

Chapter 1

1. Michael C. Davis contends that "genuine local autonomy" for Tibet is possible through Article 31 of China's Constitution, which allows the state to establish a "special administrative region when necessary." In Davis' view, this would provide a more flexible and constructive solution to China's problems with Tibet. Yedor contends that the Dalai Lama has not given up the quest for independence for Tibet, despite his call for a "middle way," which Yedor asserts "goes against the Chinese Constitution and law." In your opinion, should China allow genuine Tibetan autonomy within China? Would this be a fair solution to the conflict?

2. According to Patrick French, the Dalai Lama should abandon the so-called "Hollywood strategy" regarding Tibet which, French contends, outrages the Chinese leadership. Instead, he should engage in "back-channel" diplomacy with China. Tibet's Communist Party chief, Zhang Qingli, contends that China should not negotiate with the Dalai Lama's Tibetan Government in Exile, which he asserts is illegitimate. In your view, should China recognize the Tibetan Government in Exile and negotiate with its leader, the Dalai Lama? Why?

3. Students for a Free Tibet contend that Tibet is a sovereign nation occupied by the repressive government of the People's Republic of China. The student group asserts the right of the Tibetan people to fight for self-determination to protect their rights and culture. Kim Petersen questions the right of Tibet to absolute self-determination and contends that it is human rights that are absolute. She also

argues the security needs of the People's Republic of China must also be considered. In your opinion, which argument is most convincing? Why?

Chapter 2

1. Lindsey Hilsum contends that China's modernizing of Tibet is a daily reminder to indigenous Tibetans of the disrespect of the Han Chinese who claim cultural superiority over them. John Makin, on the other hand, asserts that the Lamaist State of Tibet is already a memory and that Tibet should focus on the future. In your view, is the Chinese government doing enough to preserve and protect Tibetan heritage and culture?

2. Abrahm Lustgarten contends that it is the tourist economy and influx of Han Chinese tourists that most threaten Tibet's unique culture. Narasimhan Ram contends that high economic growth engendered by tourist dollars—particularly with the opening of the Quinghai-Tibet railway—will help to "overcome the historical backwardness" of the Tibetan plateau. In what ways, in your view, can a tourist economy benefit Tibet's traditional culture?

3. China's rule threatens the free and open practice of Tibetan Buddhism according to Frank Ching, but Shi Shan contends that Chinese Buddhism is threatened by the Dalai Lama and his political ambitions put under the guise of Buddhism and peace. In your opinion, could Tibetan Buddhism ever flourish under Chinese rule? Is the Dalai Lama a threat to Chinese Buddhism?

Chapter 3

1. Kevin Jiang argues that China provides economic development, such as the construction of the Qinghai-Tibet railway line, that will provide many opportunities for Tibet. He believes Tibet will become strengthened under Chinese rule. One H.E.A.R.T. (Health, Education and Research,

Tibet), a medical relief organization dedicated to the health and well-being of Tibetan women and children, contends that women and children on the Tibetan Plateau continue to suffer from inadequate medical access and support, despite Tibet's improved infrastructure and economic advancements supported by the Chinese Central Government. In your opinion, are the Tibetan people, particularly the women and children, being fairly served under Chinese rule? Should China subsidize Tibetan development?

2. The Tibetan Children's Education and Welfare Fund, a part of the Dalai Lama's Central Tibetan Administration, contends that Tibetans in exile must have access to a traditional Tibetan education, one that recognizes education not merely as a means of livelihood, but also a means of achieving temporary, as well as long-term, welfare for the self and others. According to the Tibetan Centre for Human Rights and Democracy (TCHRD), Tibetans seeking education within Tibet, particularly young girls, may be ineligible to apply for higher studies if they fail to score good marks in Chinese languages tests. This restriction, the organization contends, has led many young girls into prostitution as a means of livelihood. What responsibility, in your opinion, does the Chinese Central Government have in assuring a fair educational opportunity for Tibetan women?

3. The United States-based, pro-Democracy organization Freedom House contends that the political and civil rights of the Tibetan people are not adequately respected by the Chinese Central Government and critics face repression. Chamba Phuntsok, governor of the People's Government of Tibet Autonomous Region, argues that with the assistance of the Chinese Central Government, the lives of

Tibetans have been transformed from serfs into masters of their fate. Which argument is the most convincing, in your opinion?

Chapter 4

1. Peter Haertling argues that the fragile ecosystem of the Tibetan plateau and the rights of the people to advocate for environmental protections will be seriously impacted by the Qinghai-Tibet Railway and the many changes it will bring to the Tibetan plateau. James C. Cobb and other geoscientists argue that sufficient engineering precautions have been put in place to safeguard the fragile ecosystem of Tibet and that the rail link from China is a positive development. In your opinion, will the Qinghai-Tibet Railway prove to be an asset to Tibet?

2. Guanli Wang argues that climate change poses the greatest threat to the ecosystem on the Tibetan plateau and, unless intercepted, will cause an ecological, economic, and social catastrophe. Patrick T. Hughes contends that it is Chinese occupation of Tibet that is responsible for the decline in the management and preservation of Tibet's natural resources. In your view, which opinion is most compelling? Why?

Organizations to Contact

The editors have compiled the following list of organizations concerned with the issues debated in this book. The descriptions are derived from materials provided by the organizations. All have publications or information available for interested readers. The list was compiled on the date of publication of the present volume; names, addresses, phone and fax numbers, and e-mail and Internet addresses may change. Be aware that many organizations take several weeks or longer to respond to inquiries, so allow as much time as possible.

All China Women's Federation (ACWF)
8610-6510355685112107 • Fax: 8610-85112107
E-mail: womenofchina@163.com
Web site: www.womenofchina.cn

The All China Women's Federation (ACWF), founded in 1949, is a social group under the leadership of the Communist Party of China (CPC). The ACWF acts to unite women from various ethnic backgrounds and circles, and works toward the further emancipation of women to represent and safeguard women's rights and interests and promote gender equality while serving as a bridge and link between the CPC, the Government of China, and all Chinese women.

Amnye Machen Institute (AMI)
Tibetan Centre for Advanced Studies, McLeod Ganj
Dharamshala (H.P.)   176219
   India
91-0189221441 • Fax: 91-0189221073
E-mail: ami@amnyemachen.org
Web site: www.amnyemachen.org

The Tibetan Centre for Advanced Studies is one of the leading institutions for the study of Tibetan language, history and culture, with an emphasis on non-Buddhist traditions. The Amnye Machen Institute (AMI) is named for the major mountain range in northeastern Tibet. The Institute's focus is on secular subjects with emphasis on the contemporary and the neglected aspects of Tibetan culture and history.

Center for Research on Tibet

Department of Anthropology
Case Western Reserve University
Cleveland, OH   44106-7125
(216) 368-2265 • Fax: (216) 368-5334
E-mail: tibet@case.edu
Web site: www.case.edu/affil/tibet/index.htm

The Center for Research on Tibet works in a collaborative relationship with the Tibet Academy of Social Sciences (TASS) in Lhasa to conceptualize and conduct research on Tibetan history, society, language, ecology/physiology and culture so as to understand traditional Tibet and the manner in which it has changed. The Center is also compiling an oral history archive of Tibetans available for online search.

China-Tibet Information Center

8610-82253922803
E-mail: e-editor@tibet.cn
Web site: www.eng.tibet.cn.

The China-Tibet Information Center is the largest multilanguage, Web-based information portal for news and opinion on China's Tibet. The Web site features articles, photos and videos on Tibet's culture, religion, history, environment, business and society from the viewpoint of the Chinese Communist Party.

International Campaign for Tibet (ICT)

825 Jefferson Place NW, Washington, DC   20036
(202) 785-1515 • Fax: (202) 785-4343
E-mail: info@savetibet.org
Web site: http://savetibet.org

The International Campaign for Tibet (ICT) was founded in 1988 to promote human rights and democratic freedoms for the people of Tibet. The ICT is a nonprofit advocacy organization that monitors and reports on human rights, environmental, and socioeconomic conditions in Tibet and promotes self-determination for the Tibetan people through negotiations between the Chinese government and the Dalai Lama.

One H.E.A.R.T. (Health, Education and Research Tibet)
352 Denver Street, Suite 350, Salt Lake City, UT   84111
(801) 596-3317 • Fax: (801) 596-1687
E-mail: Info@OneHeartTibet.org
Web site: www.onehearttibet.org

One H.E.A.R.T. (Health, Education and Research Tibet) is a not-for-profit group headquartered in Salt Lake City, Utah. One H.E.A.R.T. operates in association with the University of Utah Health Services Center and in partnership with the Lhasa Prefecture Health Bureau in Tibet and the Chinese Center for Disease Control in Beijing. The organization acts to provide health care education and assistance to underserved Tibetan women and children through culturally sensitive training programs for rural health workers and community members that introduce life-saving childbirth skills to help women and children survive.

Students for a Free Tibet (SFT)
602 East Fourteenth Street, 2nd Floor, New York, NY
(212) 358-0071 • Fax: (212) 358-1771
E-mail: info@studentsforafreetibet.org
Web site: www.studentsforafreetibet.org

Students for a Free Tibet (SFT) is a chapter-based worldwide network of young people and activists working through education, grassroots organizing, and nonviolent direct action in solidarity with the Tibetan people in their struggle for political freedom and independence. SFT acts to empower and train youth as leaders in the worldwide movement for social justice.

Tibetan Children's Education & Welfare Fund
Department of Education, Gangchen Kyishong
Dharamsala, District Kangra, Himachal Pradesh   176215
  India
91-01892222721/222572 • Fax: 91-01892223481
E-mail: webmaster@tcewf.org

The Tibetan Children's Educational & Welfare Fund is a registered society of the Department of Education of the Central Tibetan Administration of His Holiness the Dalai Lama in Dharamsala, India. The organization functions to provide Tibetan students in exile with adequate care, an appropriate educational foundation and the opportunity for higher study within the principles outlined in the Basic Education Policy for Tibetans in Exile.

Tibet Conservation Fund
1145 Seventeenth Street NW, Washington, DC   20036
(800) 373-1717 • Fax: (202) 429-5709
E-mail: givinginfo@ngs.org
Web site: www.nationalgeographic.com

A project of the National Geographic Society's Research, Conservation, and Exploration grant-making programs, the Tibet Conservation Fund supports work to preserve the biological diversity of Tibet and to help scientists, explorers, local residents, and government officials work together to preserve Tibet's wildlife and habitat, as well as to support conservation efforts in surrounding regions where Tibetan communities reside.

Tibet Information Network
c/o Thierry DodinDorotheenstr, Bonn   12453111
  Germany
44-02030020633 • Fax: 49-022389494466
E-mail:tin@tibetinfonet.net
Web site: www.tibetinfonet.net

Tibet Information Network is an international decentralized network of Tibetans and non-Tibetan individuals with expert knowledge on the issues facing contemporary Tibet. It is an independent and nonprofit information source that monitors the situation in Tibet and attempts to present in-depth, well-informed reports to Tibetan and Chinese communities, and others who seek an understanding of the complex social, political, cultural and ecological issues that shape the daily lives of contemporary Tibetans.

Tibetan Children's Education Foundation (TCEF)
PO Box 1403, Helena, MT 59624
E-mail: hope@tibetanchildrenseducation.org
Web site: www.tibetanchildrenseducation.org

The Tibetan Children's Education Fund (TCEF) is a charitable educational corporation dedicated to Tibetan children. The United States-based nonprofit organization focuses on the education of Tibetan children in exile and the preservation of the threatened Tibetan culture with an emphasis on preservation of sacred arts. TCEF also organizes cultural exchange programs.

Tibetan Centre for Human Rights and Democracy (TCHRD)
Top Floor, Narthang Building, Gangchen Kyishong
Dharamsala, H.P.   176215
    India
91-1892223363 • Fax: 91-1892225874
E-mail: dsala@tchrd.org
Web site: www.tchrd.org

The Tibetan Centre for Human Rights and Democracy (TCHRD) is a Tibetan nongovernmental organization (NGO) that investigates the human rights situation in Tibet and presents this information internationally through forums and other educational programs. TCHRD acts to promote the principles of democracy within the Tibetan community.

Tibet Environment Watch (TEW)
E-mail: info@tew.org
Web site: www.tew.org

Tibet Environmental Watch (TEW) is an online information source for up-to-date news of environmental conditions in Tibet and also provides information and support for the Dalai Lama's vision of the Tibetan plateau as a "zone of peace—a free refuge where humanity and nature can live in peace and in harmonious balance."

Tibetan Youth Congress (TYC)
Central Executive Committee, P.O., Mcleod Ganj
Dharamsala (H.P.) 176219
   India
91-1892221554/221239 • Fax: 91-1892221849
E-mail: tyc@vsnl.com
Web site: www.tibetanyouthcongress.org

The Tibetan Youth Congress (TYC) is an independent nongovernmental organization founded by Tibetans in exile with over thirty thousand members worldwide in eighty-one regional branches. TYC is dedicated to promoting and protecting Tibetan national unity and is united in the struggle for complete independence for the whole of Tibet. TYC does not subscribe to any particular political ideology or to any particular religion or religious sect.

Bibliography of Books

Jane Ardley

The Tibetan Independence Movement: Political, Religious and Gandhian Perspectives. London; New York: RoutledgeCurzon, 2002.

Robert Barnett

Lhasa: Streets with Memories. New York: Columbia University Press, 2006.

Helen R. Boyd

The Future of Tibet: The Government-in-Exile Meets the Challenge of Democratization. New York: Peter Lang, 2004.

Alex Butler

Feminism, Nationalism, and Exiled Tibetan Women. New Delhi: Kali for Women, 2003.

Mayank Chhaya

Dalai Lama: Man, Monk, Mystic. New York: Doubleday, 2007.

Erik D. Curren

Buddha's Not Smiling: Uncovering Corruption at the Heart of Tibetan Buddhism Today. Alaya Press: 2005.

Dalai Lama XIV

The Essential Dalai Lama, ed. Rajiv Mehrotra. Toronto: Penguin Books Canada, 2005.

Mike Dunham

Buddha's Warriors: The Story of the CIA-Backed Tibetan Freedom Fighters, the Chinese Communist Invasion, and the Ultimate Fall of Tibet. New York: Jeremy P. Tarcher & Penguin, 2004.

Patrick French — *Tibet, Tibet: A Personal History of a Lost Land.* New York: Knopf, Random House, Inc., 2003.

J.B. Heath — *Tibet and China in the Twenty-first Century: Non-violence Versus State Power.* London: Saqi, 2005.

Ashild Kolas and Monika P. Thowsen — *On the Margins of Tibet: Cultural Survival on the Sino-Tibetan Frontier.* Seattle: University of Washington Press, 2005.

Thomas Laird — *The Story of Tibet: Conversations with the Dalai Lama.* New York: Grove Press, 2006.

Dawa Norbu — *Tibet: The Road Ahead.* London: Rider, 2000.

Francoise Pommaret — *Tibet, an Enduring Civilization.* New York: Abrams Discoveries Series, 2003.

John Powers — *History as Propaganda: Tibetan Exiles Versus the People's Republic of China.* New York: Oxford University Press, 2004.

Morris Rossabi, ed. — *Governing China's Multiethnic Frontiers.* Seattle: University of Washington Press, 2004.

Barry Sautman and June Teufel Dreyer, eds. — *Contemporary Tibet: Politics, Development, and Society in a Disputed Region.* New York: M.E. Sharpe, 2006.

Warren W. Smith   *China's Tibet: Autonomy or Assimilation?* Boulder, CO: Rowman and Littlefield, 2007.

Zhang, Xiaoming   *China's Tibet.* Beijing: China Intercontinental Press, 2004.

Index

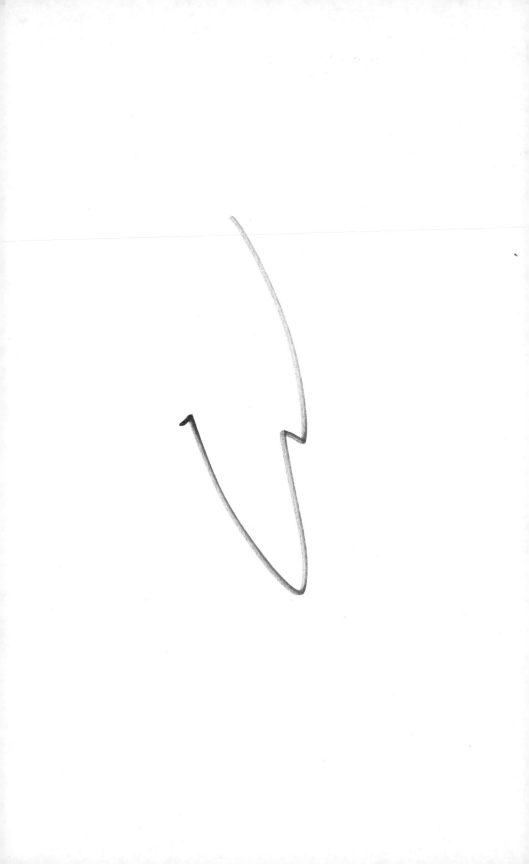